TIDE ROLLS

Alabama's 2011 National Championship Season

Text by Kirk McNair
Photography by Stuart McNair

NATIONAL CHAMPIONSHIP
Mercedes-Benz Superdome
BAKER
22
CLAIBORNE
17

This book is available in quantity at special discounts for your group or organization.
For further information, contact:

Triumph Books LLC
542 South Dearborn Street, Suite 750
Chicago, Illinois 60605
(312) 939-3330
Fax (312) 663-3557
www.triumphbooks.com

Printed in U.S.A.
ISBN: 978-1-60078-735-5

Content packaged by Mojo Media, Inc.
Joe Funk: Editor
Jason Hinman: Creative Director

Additional photography by Butch Dill

Contents

Introduction

There is something special about every national championship, even for a program like Alabama that has celebrated "We're No. 1" on numerous occasions.

The count is now 14 after the Crimson Tide defense smothered previously No. 1 LSU, 21–0, in the BCS National Championship Game at the Louisiana Superdome in New Orleans.

Quite a few of Alabama's national championships have been of the undefeated, untied variety, and those are probably best. The 2011 Crimson Tide provides a bit of a trivia lore: What Alabama national championship team went 11–1 but defeated every team it faced?

Indeed, the one loss to LSU in regular season play on November 5 in Tuscaloosa's Bryant-Denny Stadium was redeemed with a BCS National Championship Game victory over the Fighting Tigers in the Louisiana Superdome in New Orleans on January 9, 2012.

As Bama's All-America/Outland Trophy winner and Academic All-America tackle Barrett Jones saw it, the Tide's win over LSU wasn't revenge. It was "restoring order."

Alabama's second BCS national championship in three years adds to the incredible Crimson Tide football history—national records of 59 bowl appearances and 33 bowl victories.

It is also another rung on Bama Coach Nick Saban's ladder to the Hall of Fame. Saban is the ultimate process man, insisting that the goal of his players and teams is only to play its best. That doesn't mean that winning the national championship is not a goal; only that Saban thinks that is best accomplished by his team playing to a high standard.

Saban will join select Bama company when he goes into the Hall of Fame at the end of his career. Wallace Wade started Alabama bowl tradition with victories in the Rose Bowl. Frank Thomas followed him and equaled Wade's achievements.

The ultimate standard bearer was Paul "Bear" Bryant, who was not at all bashful about the national championship being his goal. He won six of them in his magnificent 25-year career as head coach at his alma mater. "If you win the national championship, everything else kind of takes care of itself," he growled.

Actually, not exactly, As wonderful as the 2011 season was, it was not a Southeastern Conference championship year for the Tide. That was a first: to win the national title but not the conference crown. Still, Alabama has 22 SEC championships, far and away the most.

Also in the Hall of Fame and also with an Alabama national championship is Gene Stallings. Like Bryant on two occasions, Stallings won his national championship in the Louisiana Superdome, a win over Miami to complete an undefeated season in 1992. Stallings was in New Orleans to see Saban win his third BCS title. Ironically, Saban won his first as head coach at LSU in 2003—in the Superdome.

The four Hall of Famers preceding Saban would all be pleased with the way the 2011 Crimson Tide won its national championship. Defense—a lost art in some football realms—is alive and well in Tuscaloosa. The performance of the 2011 Crimson Tide goes down with the goal-line stand Bama of 1978 and the beat-down of Miami in 1992, two of the four national titles Bama has won in the Louisiana Superdome.

There was a vocal minority who thought Alabama did not belong in the national championship game because of its regular season loss to LSU. There were postulations that the championship might be split if Bama defeated LSU. When it was over, there was only silence from the critics and only one national champion. ∎

Jordan Jefferson and the LSU offense had trouble getting anything going against Alabama's No. 1-ranked defense.

Alabama Dominates LSU For Crown

In a game that LSU Coach Les Miles predicted would be "big-boy football," it was men against boys as Alabama stood up to win the national championship Monday night. The Crimson Tide's defense held the Fighting Tigers to almost nothing and although the Bama offense was mostly field goals, it was more than enough.

January 9

Alabama 21

LSU 0

In a game in which many had criticized the presence of Alabama, the Crimson Tide dominated in winning its second national championship in three years and 14th overall.

Bama was a convincing 21–0 winner over LSU in the BCS National Championship Game at the Louisiana Superdome in New Orleans.

Alabama finishes the season 12–1 and was able to avenge its only loss of the year at the hands of LSU. The Tigers had been 13–0 before the loss.

Jeremy Shelley kicked five field goals and Trent Richardson went 34 yards for a touchdown that absolutely iced the game in the fourth quarter, but the lion's share of credit goes to Alabama's defense and to first-year starting quarterback A.J. McCarron.

And, of course, to Nick Saban and his coaching staff. It is Saban's third BCS championship as a coach—one at LSU and two at Alabama.

Alabama could say it left points on the field.

LSU never came close to scoring. The Tigers made only one foray into Alabama territory, that in the final eight minutes of the fourth quarter, and by the time the series had ended the ball was back at midfield in Alabama's possession.

For most of the game it was field goals—mostly made field goals by Shelley—as had been the case in the first Alabama-LSU game this season. As in the first game, won by LSU 9–6 in overtime, there were five field goals. But in that game, three were by LSU and two by Alabama. Monday night, all were by the Crimson Tide.

It was 3–0 after one quarter, 9–0 at halftime, 15–0 going to the fourth quarter, and 21–0 when Richardson took it in from 34 yards out with 4:36 to play. That turned the steady exit of purple and gold from the stands into a torrent.

It appeared from the start that Alabama followers were no worse than even and perhaps in a slight majority of the 78,237 in attendance.

Alabama scored three points on the final

Trey Depriest and the rest of Alabama's defense kept the Tigers bottled up all four quarters.

play of the first half and then took the second-half kickoff and drove to another field goal and a 12–0 lead.

Shelley was mostly good on field goals, but missed a couple that would have provided breathing room. He also missed the extra point following the lone touchdown scored in eight quarters and an overtime between Alabama and LSU this season.

Sophomore quarterback A.J. McCarron was selected as the offensive player of the game as he completed 23 of 34 passes for 234 yards with no interceptions. Courtney Upshaw, who led the Tide with seven tackles (six unassisted) and had one sack, was the defensive MVP.

The statistical discrepancy was even greater than the final score. Alabama had 21 first downs to five for LSU. The Tide had 35 rushes for 150 yards, the Tigers 27 carries for 39 yards. McCarron's passing totals compared to LSU quarterback Jordan Jefferson's 11 of 17 for 53 yards. Jefferson suffered an interception and was sacked four times. McCarron was sacked twice, but did not have an interception.

Alabama's total offense was 69 plays for 384 yards, LSU's 44 plays for 92 yards. Bama had one fumble recovery and one interception and the Tide did not have a turnover. Alabama had only one penalty, an offsides on the final LSU punt of the game.

Almost everyone expected LSU to have an advantage in the kicking game. That didn't happen. Alabama's Cody Mandell punted three times for a 44.3 average and allowed a total of one return for one yard. LSU's Brad Wing, the All-Southeastern Conference punter, kicked nine times for a 45.7 average, but the Tide had three returns for 67 yards.

Alabama owned the time of possession statistic, 35:26 to 24:34.

Richardson had a solid rushing game, made particularly good by his 34-yard touchdown run in the fourth quarter. He had 20 carries for 96 yards. Eddie Lacy had 11 carries for 43 yards.

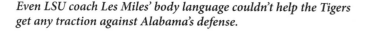

Even LSU coach Les Miles' body language couldn't help the Tigers get any traction against Alabama's defense.

Kenny Bell had only one catch in the game, but it went for 26 yards and opened up the LSU defense in the first drive of the second half.

Marquis Maze was injured early in the game on a 49-yard punt return and his place was taken by Kevin Norwood, who had four catches for 78 yards. Brad Smelley had seven catches for 39 yards and Darius Hanks five for 58.

Christion Jones replaced Maze on punt and kickoff returns and had a 15 yard punt return and ran back the only LSU kickoff of the game for 32 yards.

An expected option offense from LSU was a non-factor. The Tigers' top rusher was Kenny Hilliard with five catches for 16 yards. Jefferson, who somewhat surprisingly went all the way at quarterback for LSU, had 14 rushes for 15 yards.

Alabama had an excellent drive to end the first half with points on the final play of the second quarter and a 9–0 lead at intermission. When Bama got the ball back on a punt at its 24 with 1:59 to play, most expected the Tide to just run out the clock and be content to get the ball to start the second half. But the reasoning on the sideline seemed to be that in a game where points may be hard to come by, go after them.

Three Trent Richardson plays got a first down at the Alabama 37. After a pass to H-back Brad Smelley lost a couple of yards, the Tide called time out with 37 seconds to play. Quarterback A.J. McCarron hit wide receiver Kevin Norwood— playing in place of an injured Marquis Maze— for a 20-yard gain into LSU territory. McCarron then connected with tight end Mike Williams for four yards, Norwood for eight, and Darius Hanks for nine to give the Tide four seconds from the LSU 24.

Jeremy Shelley nailed his third field goal of the first half from 41 yards as the half ended for the 9–0 advantage.

The first score of the game was set up by an unlikely event, but had a familiar ring of field goal. LSU had given up six total yards on punt returns all season. On Brad Wing's second punt of the night, a 54-yard boot, Bama's Marquis Maze took the ball at his 25 and returned it up the middle, then down the right sidelines to the LSU 26. Bama got 16 yards on a first down pass from A.J. McCarron to Darius Hanks to the 10.

Kicker Jeremy Shelley tied a bowl record with five field goals, redeeming himself for his critical misses in the regular season tilt against LSU.

There the drive stalled and Jeremy Shelley kicked a 23-yard field goal with five minutes remaining in the first quarter.

Shelley made it 6–0 with a second quarter 34-yard field goal. Bama drove 58 yards in 11 plays to the score. McCarron completed first down passes of nine yards to Darius Hanks for a first down and Richardson had first-down runs of seven and 20 yards for first downs to set up the kick.

Alabama also missed a scoring opportunity. The Tide drove from its 11 to the LSU 32 in a drive that started at the end of the first quarter and went into the second quarter. McCarron had a first-down pass to Eddie Lacy and Lacy had first-down runs of nine and three yards before McCarron connected with Norwood (who made an excellent leaping catch near the sideline) for 26 yards.

It appeared the Tide's Cade Foster would attempt a 49-yard field goal, but a fake—a shovel pass from holder McCarron to tight end Chris Underwood—got the first down. Unfortunately for Bama, the Tide couldn't move and tried to settle for a 42-yard Shelley field goal, but it was blocked by LSU's Michael Brockers.

After taking a 9–0 first half lead, the Tide had an explosive drive that ended in a bit of disappointment by not getting a touchdown. Christion Jones returned the second half kick-off to the 32. McCarron hit Darius Hanks for 19 and Kenny Bell for 26 and in two plays Bama had moved to the LSU 23. But three plays came up short of the first down and Shelley kicked his fourth field goal of the game, a 35-yard effort with barely two minutes gone in the third quarter. It was 12–0.

LSU seemed to be making an offensive threat when the Tigers moved to a first down at the LSU 43, but an Upshaw sack thwarted the effort and Wing was punting again.

McCarron connected with Norwood for 24 yards and a first down at midfield, but the Tide quarterback then missed on a wide-open Hanks and the Tide had to punt.

The offense didn't have to wait long for another chance, but it was perhaps the most disappointing opportunity of

By the time Trent Richardson rumbled in for a fourth-quarter touchdown—the first scored by either team after eight quarters of play this season—the win was all but sealed for the Crimson Tide.

the night. Under pressure, Jefferson tried to shovel a pass to Spencer Ware, and the ball went to Bama linebacker C.J. Mosley, who was tackled by Jefferson at the LSU 27. There was a long delay because Mosley suffered an apparent knee injury and had to be carted from the field to the medical examination room.

Presented that opportunity, the Tide could muster only four yards in three plays. Shelley had a 41-yard opportunity, but he pushed it just outside the right upright and Bama had squandered a nice scoring opportunity.

After another LSU punt—the Tigers were good on only two of 12 third down conversions and had six three-and-outs among its 11 possessions—Alabama got another start from midfield. Lacy had back-to-back 11-yard runs to move into the Red Zone. As had been the case earlier, the drive stalled and Shelley was called on for a 44-yard field goal, which he nailed to make it 15–0.

Mandell's final punt of the night was a beauty, a 52-yarder to All-America Tyrann Mathieu at the 34. Mathieu returned it for one yard, then was smothered by Bama's Dre Kirkpatrick who handled Mathieu roughly. That may have been a little payback for the cheap shot Mathieu had against Kirkpatrick in the first game of the season.

LSU did follow that with its one trip into Alabama territory, but going for it on fourth-and-18, Jefferson was hit by Dont'a Hightower and fumbled, the ball recovered by Nick Gentry.

Only 6:15 remained. McCarron had a nice little run of 13 yards and from the 34 Richardson took the ball at left end and went untouched to the end zone. Although Shelley's extra point kick hit the right upright and was no good, it was 21–0 and the game was over.

The celebration in a town that knows how to celebrate was just beginning for those in crimson and white. ∎

Trent Richardson ran for 96 bruising yards on 20 carries in the biggest game of his college career.

McCarron Cements Place In History

— By Cary L. Clark

Like Greg McElroy, Jay Barker, Steadman Shealy, Jeff Rutledge, and Joe Namath before him, Alabama quarterback A.J. McCarron cemented his Bama quarterback legacy in the BCS Championship Game. McCarron, a first-year starter, took his Crimson Tide to its 14th national title before a sold out crowd in the Louisiana Superdome in New Orleans.

The Alabama sophomore led the Tide to a 21–0 win over LSU by completing 23 of 34 passes for 234 yards. He was named offensive game MVP in the process and piloted an offense that out-gained its opponent 384 yards to 92.

"I've been dreaming of this my whole life," McCarron said just after his team's shellacking of previous No. 1 LSU. "This is a blessing for my teammates and my parents. I never thought, starting football at the age of four, I would be here. Coming into the season and not knowing if I was going to be the starter, and Coach [Nick Saban] gave the job to me."

Gave it?

"I felt like I earned it," McCarron said. "It showed the confidence [Saban had in me]. When I first got recruited here, I told him I would lead him to a national championship. No one can ever take that away from me."

As always, McCarron was quick to compliment his teammates. One example: Kevin Norwood, who came off the bench for an injured Marquis Maze to catch four balls for 78 yards.

"We didn't have that happen all year [in a game]," McCarron said of Norwood's performance, "but when we rotate in and out [receivers] during practice, and when we see that happen all year long, every day of the week [in practice], guys step up and make plays for us."

McCarron was sacked twice, but had time to throw nearly every time he dropped back. "The offensive line gave me time," he said. "And the receivers, I just put it in their area and those guys went up and made a bunch of plays tonight for me. You can't say enough about that group."

Other receivers who stepped up in Maze's absence included a pair of seniors playing their final game in crimson: H-back Brad Smelley, who caught a game-high seven balls for 39 yards, and wide receiver Darius Hanks (five catches, 58 yards).

AJ McCarron joins the ranks of legendary Alabama quarterbacks to win a national title, and celebrates the team's final ranking with Crimson Tide fans.

Sophomore quarterback A.J. McCarron completed 23 of 34 passes for 234 yards and no interceptions in leading the Tide to victory.

McCarron said his eyes lit up a bit when he saw that the game plan for the title tilt called for him to throw the ball more than usual. "I was very thankful, first of all, about it," he said. "We've been leaning on No. 3 [Trent Richardson] all year. He's our main guy. We knew coming into the game somebody else had to step up, and Coach Saban just gave me the opportunity. When you have a group of receivers like I have, it makes your job easy as a quarterback. They go up and make plays for you and make you look like a hero. It all falls back on those guys and that offensive line for giving me time."

McCarron said he had no problem keeping his motivation up for 60 minutes this go-around as opposed to having played more laid-back in the 9–6 loss to the Tigers on November 5.

"During the Florida game, I'm pretty sure most of the country saw Coach Saban rip me for showing too much emotion. After the LSU game, the first time, he told me to play like myself, and show more emotion."

Saban quickly chimed in.

"Let me correct that," said the coach. "I just didn't want to have to pull that big [Florida] guy you were ready to get into it with off of you."

Continuing, McCarron said, "So Coach told me to show some emotion, play like myself. I'm just thankful Coach gave me the opportunity to come out and put the ball in my hands and make some plays.

"I think a bunch of our success goes to the guys that don't really get [publicity], that people don't see, the defensive scout team. Those guys gave us a perfect look all week long for the past 44 days we've been practicing for LSU. Those guys have been perfect on that side of the ball during practice. Those are the guys that don't ever get noticed in the newspapers, and they earned this [BCS Championship] as much as everybody else that played in the game tonight."

Senior jack linebacker Courtney Upshaw earned defensive MVP honors on the strength of seven tackles and a sack. "We knew they were going to come out and try to run the ball against us," he said. "We really didn't call many blitzes. We were just hoping to contain them. We were mostly able to do what we planned.

"We wanted to go out and execute, especially against the option. We were able to do that, and it was a big part of us winning this game."

Upshaw said he and his team enjoyed coming in as an underdog in the minds of many national pundits. "We knew a lot of people said we didn't belong here, that LSU was going to run the ball down our throats," he said. "But as a defense, we were able to execute and get the win. I'm happy and proud to be a part of Alabama. It feels good to get the win." ∎

Even after winning another national title, coach Nick Saban already seems focused on next season.

Trent Richardson proudly displays a hometown paper proclaiming the Crimson Tide No. 1 in all the land.

Saban Wants Action, Not Intention

Consistency. Mental energy. Focus. Perseverance. Intensity. Mental toughness. In the heat of football fall camp, those are more than just words being used around the Alabama football scene.

Alabama Coach Nick Saban put his team through a two-hour practice in the heat of Tuscaloosa Thursday, a day after the Tide had gone through two practices on Wednesday. Moreover, there's a scrimmage just ahead, on Saturday.

"It's not what your intention is," Saban said. "It's what your action is. And everybody controls his own actions by what he does."

Alabama had its eighth practice of fall camp Thursday. The Crimson Tide is working towards the season-opener against Kent State in Bryant-Denny Stadium on September 3.

"The focus for us right now is playing with consistency," Saban said. "We need to get everybody out there on a daily basis having the kind of focus, mental energy, and intensity that you need to improve, so you can play winning football at your position. You have to have lots of mental toughness to be able to persevere under the circumstances that we are in, but everyone that we are playing against is in the same situation. It is hot everywhere. Everybody controls their own actions by what they do. That is what we need to continue to

do as an entire team, not one part of the team one day, another part of the team the next day.

"Everybody's got to have that kind of mental energy and intensity all the time to improve. Every day you go out there, you get better or you get worse, you don't stay the same.

"I see improvement in some areas of the team but I don't see it with the kind of consistency that we need, because that's what creates a dependability and trust that everybody has in each other."

Saban said he would be looking for those attributes when the Crimson Tide goes to Bryant-Denny Stadium Saturday for the first of two pre-season scrimmage practices.

He said he would look to see "who can go out there and play with the kind of consistency and play winning football at their position? Who can persevere and have the mental toughness and discipline to do their job? I think we need to find that out about a lot of our players. Some players around here have done that in the past. It might not be as critical for them as it is for the younger guys who have a chance to contribute to the team."

If Nick Saban seemed extra focused going into the 2011 season, it was because he knew that his Crimson Tide had the chance to be one of the most spectacular teams in school history.

"Every ball that hits the ground in practice, our guys have to scoop and score." — Nick Saban

One area Saban hopes to see improvement this year is Alabama's defense causing fumbles. An embarrassing statistic from last year is that Bama ranked 118th in the nation in causing fumbles. There are only 120 teams in the Tide's division.

To some extent, Alabama is not changing its force fumble drills.

"We did it last year," he said. "We always do. But we are getting more in camp and we are emphasizing it. Players are more aware of it. We do a turnover circuit once every three practices for every player on defense. We're constantly emphasizing stripping it and getting it out, effort getting to the ball.

"You never know when those kind of opportunities are going to occur. Every ball that hits the ground in practice, our guys have to scoop and score, whether it's a fumble, an incomplete pass or whatever it is.

"We did this last year. When we went to visit the Saints, they were one of the top teams in the NFL in turnover ratio.

"We got lots of interceptions, we just didn't get very many caused fumbles and fumble recoveries, so that's something we need to improve on. But the [2009] national championship team didn't get that many either; we only had seven, which is a whole lot better than two or whatever we got last year. That wasn't what it needs to be and we need to improve on it.

Saban demanded excellence all around him in 2011, as not even this official could escape his desire for perfection. His players worked hard all year to live up to their potential, another crowning moment in Saban's illustrious career.

"I think [Dont'a Hightower is] the guy, because most of the other guys look up to him."
— Nick Saban

"We also need to improve on our ball security on offense. Needless to say, fumbles really had an impact on the outcome of our season."

Saban was asked about the difference in Dont'a Hightower apparently being recovered from the knee injury that ended his season early in 2009. (Ironically, the question came on a day when Hightower missed practice with a hand injury that required a surgical procedure.)

Saban said, "Last year he didn't feel 100 per cent. I think he worried about the injury, that he would get injured again. think that's really all behind him. I really started to see the last two or three games of the year, where he was playing a little bit more like Dont'a of old. Certainly the bowl game looked that way.

"He has done a great job this offseason. His body fat is way down, his muscle mass is way up. He's quicker and faster and more explosive in pass rush. I think he's the guy, because most of the other guys look up to him."

As part of his Thursday post-practice report, Saban discussed injuries, including Hightower missing practice. "He'll probably be ready to come back and practice tomorrow," Saban said. "He doesn't even know how he did it."

Also missing was center William Vlachos, who was ill. Defensive end Undra Billingsley was hospitalized with illness earlier this week and has not returned. Freshman offensive lineman Ryan Kelly "is day-to-day," Saban said. "When these guys get concussions, we're very cautious on when they can come back and play." ∎

Now one of the deans of college football coaches, Saban has earned a reputation for hard-working, competitive teams. In essence, his squads are a mirror image of their head coach.

Alabama, Saban Could Not Help It

Nick Saban didn't want to run it up against Michigan State, either. There were any number of reasons for Alabama not to rout Kent State, a member of the Mid-American Conference serving as the sacrificial lamb to start the 2011 Crimson Tide season.

September 3

Alabama 48

vs Kent State 7

For starters, Alabama Coach Nick Saban played for Kent State and is a graduate of that Ohio university. For another, Kent State players spent time in Tuscaloosa this summer helping in recovery efforts following the April 27 tornado.

But some things can't be helped. There's a reason Kent State had a new head coach this year. And while Bama had some concerns about not knowing what to expect from the Golden Flashes because of new coaches and coordinators from last year, it went about as expected in Bryant-Denny Stadium Saturday.

Alabama looked like a team that has the players capable of contending for the national championship. Kent State had breakdowns in every phase of the game before making a first down.

Alabama finished off the Golden Flashes, 48–7, to open the 2011 season.

It was Alabama's second consecutive game against teams Saban had a connection to. Saban's first head-coaching job was at Michigan State. In the final game of the 2010 season, Bama defeated Michigan State, 49–7, at the Capital One Bowl in Orlando.

Alabama's domination of Kent State was complete. Even with second- and third-team players seeing plenty of action, Bama's 72 plays netted 482 yards and the Golden Flashes had 70 plays for 90 yards.

Kent finished with negative rushing yardage—23 carries for minus-9 yards—as the Tide defense had four sacks for 31 yards in losses and three other tackles for losses of 23 yards.

Alabama had 24 first downs to six for Kent State. Bama had 35 rushes for 183 yards and quarterbacks completed 21 of 37 passes for 199 yards. Kent State quarterback Keith Spencer completed 20 of 47 passes for 99 yards, a long pass of only 13 yards. He had one touchdown and one interception.

Alabama was six-for-six in red-zone scores.

A negative for the Tide was giving up four interceptions. Another was not causing one fumble, which had reportedly been a point of emphasis for the defense in spring practice and fall camp.

Trent Richardson barrels into the end zone from a yard out. The Kent State defense had no answer as Richardson kicked off his Heisman campaign with three scores on just 13 carries.

Third tailback Jalston Fowler came in for a few late carries and finished as the game's leading rusher with four carries for 69 yards and a touchdown (on a 49-yard run). Trent Richardson scored three rushing touchdowns on his 13 carries for 37 yards. Eddie Lacy had eight carries for 58 yards and a touchdown.

A.J. McCarron completed 14 of 23 passes for 226 yards and one touchdown. Phillip Sims completed 7-of-14 for 7 yards and no touchdowns. Both were intercepted twice.

Marquis Maze led Tide receivers with eight catches for 118 yards and one touchdown.

Alabama's leading tacklers against Kent State were true freshman linebacker Trey DePriest with 10 tackles (3 solos), linebacker Courtney Upshaw with seven (4 solos), including 1.5 tackles for loss and half of a quarterback sack; linebacker Dont'a Hightower with 7 tackles, half of a tackle for loss, and half of a quarterback sack; cornerback Dequan Menzie with six tackles (3 solos), 1.5 tackles for loss and half of a quarterback sack; and defensive back/linebacker Vinnie Sunseri with six tackles (3 solos).

With A.J. McCarron opening at quarterback for the Tide, Bama wasted no time in opening up a lead. Marquis Maze returned a punt 27 yards to the Kent State 36 and it took just eight plays and 3:29 until Trent Richardson had his first rushing touchdown of the year. Richardson took it in from the one and Jeremy Shelley kicked the extra point for Alabama's 7–0 lead with 10:22 remaining in the first quarter. McCarron had three completions in as many tries—two to DeAndrew White for 18 total yards and one to Maze for nine yards.

Less than two and a half minutes later McCarron completed a 24-yard post pattern pass to Maze for a 14–0 lead. The big play in the four-down, 74-yard march was a screen pass to back-up tailback Eddie Lacy for 48 yards.

Maze had several nice punt returns, including a 15-yard scamper to set Bama up at Kent State's 34 with 1:24 remaining in the first quarter. Phillip Sims took over at quarterback, as had been arranged in the three-series plan. and took just 58 seconds to make it 21–0. Lacy ran for 20 yards, Sims hit

Tyshon Goode was one of eight Golden Flashes with a reception against Alabama, but he paid the price for going over the middle in an attempt to make a grab.

White for 10, and after a formation penalty, Richardson ran it over left tackle for a nine-yard touchdown.

Alabama wasted a nice opportunity from inside the Kent State 20 in the final minutes of the first half. When the march bogged down, the Tide had to settle for a 36-yard Shelley field goal and a 24–0 lead.

Cade Foster's 53-yard field goal effort on the final play of the first half was wide right.

Alabama lost its shutout following a Sims interception. He was picked off by Norman Wolfe at the Kent 40 and returned 37 yards to the Crimson Tide 3. Two plays later Spencer Keith completed a touchdown pass to tight end Justin Thompson for the touchdown. Freddy Cortez kicked the extra point to close the gap to 24–7.

The first down play following the interception was the first of the game for Kent State in Alabama territory. Ironically, the next time Kent State was in Alabama territory was when a McCarron pass went off the hands of tight end Michael Williams and was intercepted by Leon Green for the Golden Flashes.

Richardson got his third touchdown of the day with 5:16 remaining in the third quarter to make it 31–7. The eight-play, 76-yard drive was directed by McCarron and included short passes to Lacy, which he turned into a 17-yard gain, and to Richardson for 16 yards to the one. Richardson took it in from the one to complete the drive in 3:57.

The offense had it pretty easy a few minutes later. A bobbled snap by the Kent State punter gave the ball to Bama at the Golden Flashes one-yard line. Lacy took it in to make it 38–7 with 4:03 to play.

Reminiscent of Lacy's late, long touchdown against Michigan State at the end of last season, Jalston Fowler, the third tailback, got the call in the opening moments of the fourth quarter. He ripped off a 14-yard run to the left side, then followed on the next play to the right side and went 49 yards for the touchdown to make it 45–7. The two-play drive took only 48 seconds and came with 13:27 remaining in the game. ■

Scanning the field ahead, big Eddie Lacy looks for more running room. Lacy solidified his spot behind Trent Richardson on the depth chart with his eight carries for 58 yards and a touchdown.

Tide Gets Road Win At Penn State

The word "efficient" comes to mind. Alabama had an error-free offense, a stifling (for the most part) defense, and good play from the special teams to pass the Crimson Tide's first real hurdle of the 2011 season. And the big surprise is that it seems Bama had settled on a quarterback earlier than expected.

September 10

Alabama 27

@ Penn State 11

Alabama sophomore A.J. McCarron played quarterback until the final seconds of the game as the Crimson Tide, ranked third in the nation, ran its record to 2–0 with a convincing 27–11 victory over 23rd ranked Penn State at Beaver Stadium in University Park, Pa., Saturday. The Nittany Lions fell to 1–1.

Alabama fell behind early and gave up a late touchdown to the Nittany Lions, but for the most part Penn State was held in check. Penn State drove to a field goal on its first possession of the game and scored a touchdown in the final two minutes of the game, but in between it was all Bama.

It was the second consecutive season the Tide had dominated the Lions in this two-game series of college football elite.

McCarron completed 19 of 31 passes for 163 yards, including the go-ahead touchdown, and did not suffer an interception.

Although Trent Richardson had his second consecutive game with less-than-glittering statistics, he did crack the 100-yard mark with 26 carries for 111 yards and two touchdowns. Eddie Lacy had 11 runs for 85 yards.

McCarron threw to eight difference receivers. Marquis Maze had four catches for 42 yards, Mike Williams three for 34 yards, Kevin Norwood three for 25 yards, Richardson four for 19, and Brad Smelley two for 18. Making one reception each were Kenny Bell (14 yards), Eddie Lacy (6), and Brandon Gibson (5).

Smelley also had official rushing yardage of 1 yard. It was actually less than that and made a critical first down by inches on a fourth-down fake-punt play. Trailing 3–0 at the time, Bama rode the momentum of that first down at the Tide 40-yard line to complete an 11-play, 69-yard drive and take the lead for good.

McCarron had back-to-back completions to Maze for 29 yards and Bell for 14 to move to the Penn State 12. Three plays later McCarron rifled a short pass to tight end Michael Williams for the touchdown. Jeremy Shelley's point after touchdown kick made it 7–3.

Trent Richardson pulls away from Penn State's vaunted defense. It was a fine day for Richardson, who carried for 111 yards and a pair of touchdowns that helped put the Nittany Lions away.

Penn State had opened the game with a 16-play, 54-yard drive that consumed half of the first quarter and ended with Evan Lewis kicking a 43-yard field goal.

Alabama tried to go back to the McCarron-to-Williams combination, but when that pass was overthrown, Bama ended up losing a touchdown opportunity and settling for a 22-yard Shelley field goal. Bama had driven to a first and goal as Richardson ran 22 yards to the Lions' 8-yard line. His first-down run gained three and then two pass plays blew up, forcing the field goal and a 10–3 lead.

In addition to McCarron suffering no interceptions, Alabama also did not have a fumble in the game. Meanwhile, Mark Barron had an interception and Dre Kirkpatrick caused two fumbles by Penn State, one recovered by Barron and one recovered by Dequan Menzie.

The first fumble caused by Kirkpatrick and recovered by Menzie at midfield was a big play in the Bama win. The takeaway came with 4:41 remaining in the first half. McCarron completed three third-down passes for first downs as the Tide drove to the Penn State 3-yard line. Richardson ran it in with just 35 seconds remaining before halftime for a 17–3 advantage.

Alabama's first two possessions after intermission were disappointing, back-to-back three-and-outs. Additionally, some poor Bama punts had given Penn State good field position. The Tide defense forced a three-and-out near midfield. the Lions' punt was taken by Maze at the Tide 5 and returned 44 yards behind nice blocks by Vinnie Sunseri and Hardie Buck.

That flip in field position helped lead to another Tide score. McCarron connected with Williams on a 24-yard gain to a first-and-goal at the Penn State 7. After Richardson picked up six yards on first down, a touchdown seemed likely. But Richardson was held for no gain and then McCarron threw an incomplete pass. Shelley's 18-yard field goal—a couple of yards shorter than an extra point kick—made it 20–3.

Lacy did the heavy lifting on Bama's final touchdown

It was a tough day for Penn State's rotating quarterbacks, facing pressure and near-interceptions all day. Rob Bolden got the bulk of the work, but completed just 11 passes for an anemic Nittany Lion offense.

A big hole opens up for Trent Richardson on his 13-yard touchdown run in the fourth quarter. He carried 26 times on the day, doubling his week 1 workload.

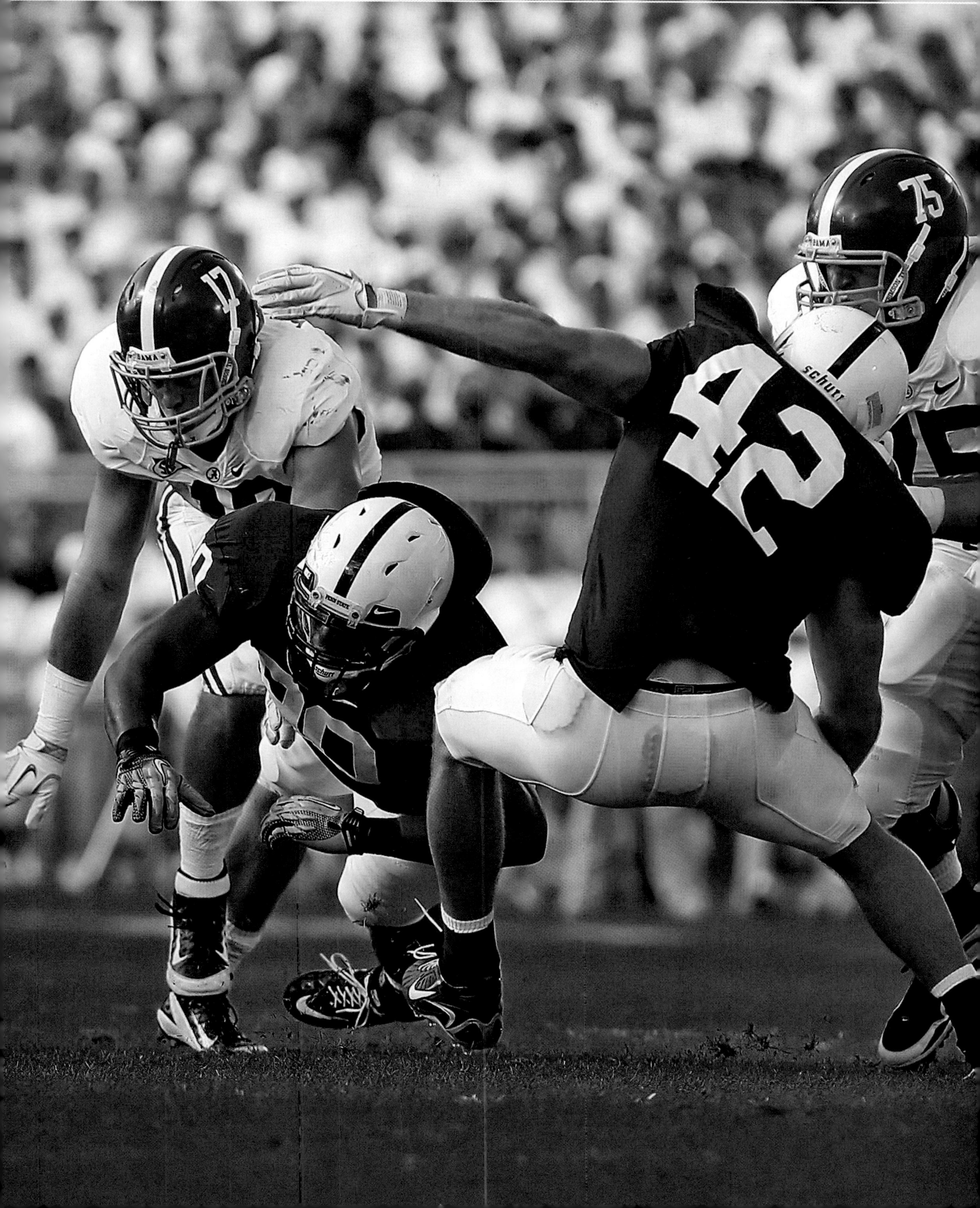

drive, but it was Richardson who picked up the touchdown. The Tide's final scoring drive was set up by Kirkpatrick's second caused fumble, this one recovered by Barron at the Tide 34.

Lacy had four consecutive runs that ate up 52 yards. The last of the four went for 30 yards to the Penn State 13. Lacy was taken out to get a breather and Richardson took advantage of getting back into the game, going 13 yards up the middle for the touchdown that made it 27–3 Bama with just over six minutes remaining in the game.

If there was a major disappointment for Alabama Coach Nick Saban, it was that Bama's defense allowed the Lions a final touchdown with a 14-play, 71-yard drive that ended with just 1:53 left in the game. Bama seemed to have held Penn State when it was third-and-20 at the Alabama 27, but quarterback Rob Bolden connected with wide receiver Shawney Kersey for 26 yards. Running back Silas Redd scored the touchdown that made it 27–11.

Barron had seven tackles (five solo) and a fumble recovery and interception to lead the Tide defensively. Linebacker C.J. Mosley was also in on seven tackles (four primary), while Menzie and Quinton Dial were in on five each.

There was not a sack in the game, although quarterbacks on both sides had to scramble a few times.

Alabama's defense allowed Penn State 251 yards on 69 plays. Of those, the Lions had 30 plays for 125 yards combined on the first and final series. On the other 10 series, Penn State managed just 39 plays for 126 yards.

Alabama finished with 41 rushes for 196 yards. With McCarron's passing, the Tide finished with 72 plays for 359 yards. Bama had an eight-minute advantage in time of possession, 34:05 to 25:55. ■

Richardson dives for the end-zone pylon, though he was eventually ruled out of bounds. The Crimson Tide were never really threatened in their first visit to Penn State since 1989.

Watkins Has Made Amazing Recoveries

The Bionic Man? Superman? The Amazing Kreskin? Alabama senior linebacker Alex Watkins brings out some interesting comparisons because of his ability to play through pain. Football players have been known to play through pain, but Watkins has taken it to a new level.

There was a thought during Alabama's spring football practice, when Alex Watkins went down with a severe knee injury, that his career might be over. He had surgery, started rehabilitation, and worked himself into shape to play his final season with the Crimson Tide.

Then against Tennessee on October 22 he suffered a broken arm. He had surgery to have a plate inserted in his left arm the next morning. Two weeks later he was playing in one of the most physical football games ever when Alabama played LSU. In fact, he played well enough to earn one of five player of the week citations from the coaching staff for his performance on special teams.

"I don't get surprised much when guys come back from injuries," Alabama Coach Nick Saban said, "but this guy never missed a day. I mean he gets his arm operated on and a plate put in his arm on Sunday, and runs out on the field on Monday like he's ready to practice.

"I said, 'Well, at least put a black (non-contact designation) shirt on so you don't get hit.'

"He didn't do a lot for a week or 10 days, but when he started feeling a little bit better, he started gradually getting back into things, and we were able to use him on special teams. We'll probably be able to continue to increase his role this week.

"Alex Watkins is an amazing guy. He has been a great leader for this group, and really cares about the team. He has done so many good things to affect other people."

Offensive guard Chance Warmack agrees that "Alex is just amazing, man. He's made player of the week twice with already a messed up knee and then he broke his arm in season. He's just a phenomenal guy. Nice person. He's just amazing. That's the best way I can put it. Amazing guy and hard worker."

Center William Vlachos said, "Tough guy. That's the epitome of toughness there. I can't imagine what it feels like, but that's obviously some toughness. I guess he doesn't feel pain if he's practicing the day after having a plate put in his arm."

Alex Watkins' arm break during the Tennessee game never slowed him down: after the bye week he was right back in the lineup against LSU.

"I've been chopping wood since I was about eight, so I guess you could count that as how I got a high tolerance for pain."

"He's like our Superman," said Tide tailback Trent Richardson. "He's got all my respect."

Watkins, a 6-3, 240-pound senior, suggests, "I guess I'm blessed. Good genes, I guess. You just fight through the pain."

Watkins took one hit during the LSU game "that hurt it. But you've got to fight through pain and play for your team. You have to block it out. You've got to do what you're capable of doing."

He hopes the 23 staples ("I counted") and the plate are removed Wednesday, which would be two and a half weeks after surgery.

He has had about an 18-minute preparation for practice with a new cast each day. The cast goes over a cushion and is then wrapped in foam padding.

Watkins said it was his first broken bone, but he knew when the Tennessee offensive lineman fell against him that the arm was fractured.

And he has known pain and surgery before. Last spring he suffered a torn ACL, a sprained MCL, nad a torn lateral meniscus.

Watkins said when he suffered the knee injury he began thinking about getting back. He didn't know if he would make it for the start of the season. "I made sure I got my rehab and was there every day to make sure I was getting better," he said.

He also thought his career might be over when he suffered the broken arm.

And he thinks the fact this is his senior season could have contributed to his resolve.

"It's very important to be on this team," he said. "Every time you go out there, you're going to be part of something great. You're playing for Alabama. Of course I want to be out there and I want to be part of that."

Fellow defensive player Josh Chapman had suggested to reporters that Watkins was able to play through the pain because he's a country boy.

"I guess you could say I was from the country," said Watkins, whose hometown is listed as Brownsville, Tennessee Actually, he said, he's from Nutbush, which limited research reveals is an unincorporated community of fewer than 300 in West Tennessee and birthplace of singer Tina Turner.

"I guess you could say it was from being from the country and a lot of stuff I do. I mean, I've been chopping wood since I was about eight, so I guess you could count that as how I got a high tolerance for pain."

Like an axe accident?

"I didn't have any accidents," he said. "Do you know how small you are at 10 or 8?"

He said his father didn't like the idea of Alex being inside playing video games. "My dad told us to go outside and chop wood. And of course it was going to be cold."

He gave reporters a little lesson in how to swing an axe to get the proper leverage.

And when he goes home, he still chops a little wood. ∎

Tough from a young age, Watkins never pouted about his injuries, instead working hard every day to make it back on the field to play in every game in 2011.

Decisive Win Was Not Very Pretty

When the No. 2 team in the nation takes on a winless team from the Sun Belt Conference, there are going to be areas of disappointment. Bama didn't get much work on punting, kickoff returns, and goal-line defense. But that doesn't mean Alabama doesn't have plenty to work on.

September 17

Alabama 41

vs North Texas 0

Alabama was expected to have little trouble with North Texas, and that was the case as the Crimson Tide rolled to a 41–0 win over the Mean Green in Bryant-Denny Stadium.

Bama's two featured running backs both had over 160 yards rushing. The Tide averaged over 10 yards per rush—33 runs for 347 yards—and had five rushing touchdowns in the contest. Trent Richardson had 11 carries for 167 yards and three touchdowns and Eddie Lacy had nine runs for 161 yards and two touchdowns.

The Crimson Tide ran its record to 3–0, while the Mean Green fell to 0–3.

Alabama didn't get to punt much against the Mean Green. Cody Mandell had only one punt. It went for just 35 yards, but that was good, because it was downed deep, at the North Texas 4.

Kickoff returns? Just one of those, too, to start the second half, and Marquis Maze ran it back a pedestrian 20 yards.

There was one nice goal-line stand in the final minutes of the game. Against Alabama back-up defenders, the Mean Green moved to a first-and-goal at the Alabama 2. Aided by a pass interference in the end zone call against the Tide, the Mean Green actually had seven plays inside the 10 and came up empty.

Disappointments included Alabama having to attempt four field goals and making only two, and scoring only three times in five red-zone trips.

Tide quarterbacks were sacked four times, while Alabama did not get a sack on the North Texas quarterbacks.

Bama emphasizes causing turnovers, but against the Mean Green there were no interceptions and no fumbles caused or recovered (North Texas did have an unforced fumble that the Mean Green recovered).

Alabama converted only 6 of 11 third-down conversions and the Mean Green had nearly a five-minute advantage in time of possession.

Alabama dominated statistically even more

Trent Richardson breaks free off left tackle to start the burst that ended in a 58-yard touchdown in the third quarter. The Crimson Tide running backs ran through holes at will against the Mean Green, averaging 10.5 yards per carry.

than on the scoreboard. The Tide had 25 first downs to 11 for North Texas. The Mean Green was held to 68 yards on 32 rushes. Alabama quarterbacks completed 21 of 29 passes with no interceptions for 239 yards. North Texas passers hit 13-of-30 for 101 yards.

Both teams ran 62 plays, with Alabama gaining 586 yards and North Texas 169.

A.J. McCarron seemed to separate himself even more from Phillip Sims in the Alabama quarterback race. McCarron completed 15 of 21 passes for 190 yards and Sims completed 6-of-8 for 49. Both quarterbacks lost fumbles, but threw no interceptions. McCarron took three sacks, Sims one.

In pass receiving, Kenny Bell had four catches for 55 yards, Brad Smelley four for 46, Brandon Gibson three for 35, and Marquis Maze three for 26.

Maze had five punt returns for 56 yards.

One of the most disappointing things about the game was Alabama's offense failing to score a touchdown after a nice opening drive. The Tide started at its 22 and drove inside the North Texas 10, but a third-down A.J. McCarron pass for Marquis Maze in the end zone was overthrown and the Tide had to settle for a 26-yard Jeremy Shelley field goal. Bama had a 3–0 lead after five minutes. McCarron had completed passes of 20 yards to Brad Smelley, 16 yards for Maze, and 11 yards to Christion Jones on the drive.

On Bama's second possession, the Tide made it 10–0 with a four-yard Trent Richardson run at left tackle. Richardson was untouched on the play. The Tide had good field position to start the drive, thanks to a 28-yard punt return by Maze to the Bama 42. The big play in the drive was a 30-yard McCarron to Christion Jones pass to the North Texas 4.

Eddie Lacy had an explosive 43-yard run in the opening moments of the second quarter to cap a six-play, 76-yard drive that took only 2:32 to increase the Alabama lead to 17–0.

The rest of the quarter was quite good on defense and unsatisfactory on offense from an Alabama standpoint. Alabama managed only a 37-yard Shelley field goal to make

Eddie Lacy scored on runs of 67 and 43 yards, part of a career-best 161 yards that came on just nine carries. He is shown here putting the finishing touches on the second-quarter carry that made it 17–0.

it 20–0 (he also missed from 36). But the Tide defense improved, which was pretty amazing considering that the Mean Green had only 15 yards of total offense in the first quarter. In the second quarter North Texas had only 10 yards of offense (on 10 rushes for 10 yards).

North Texas didn't get into Alabama territory until the third quarter, when a nice march ended with Robert Lester deflecting a 42-yard field goal try by the Mean Green's Zach Olen.

Bama was somewhat lethargic until just over nine and a half minutes remaining in the third quarter when Tent Richardson followed a Chance Warmack block at left end and went 58 yards for a touchdown. The run would have been longer except that the North Texas punter had shanked the ball out of bounds at the Alabama 42 just prior to Richardson's run.

On the first play of the fourth quarter, Shelley missed a 42-yard field goal try to leave the score at Alabama 27, North Texas 0.

Following a North Texas punt that was fair caught at the Alabama 29, it took just one play to get another Richardson touchdown. Phillip Sims came in at quarterback and kept it simple. Richardson took the handoff at right tackle, then cut straight up field on a 71-yard touchdown run that made it 34–0.

Although most of the first offense was still in a few minutes later when North Texas punted to Bama at the Tide 33, it was Phillip Sims handing off to Eddie Lacy. Lacy went 67 yards for a touchdown to make it 41–0.

Alabama's goal-line stand came in the final five minutes.

Safeties led Bama defensively. Will Lowery and Mark Barron were in on seven tackles each and Vinnie Sunseri was in on six tackles. ■

Lance Dunbar ended up rushing for more than 1,100 yards in 2011, but he wasn't able to average a yard per carry against Alabama. Josh Chapman is shown here dropping Dunbar behind the line of scrimmage.

Win Over Hogs Good Start To SEC Play

There is something of a test to playing the Southeastern Conference opener against a solid contender, particularly after games against three relatively soft opponents to start the season. That was the case for Alabama and Arkansas at Bryant-Denny Stadium. Bama passed the test with flying colors.

September 24

Alabama 38

vs Arkansas 14

Alabama, ranked second in the nation, defeated Arkansas, 38–14, to improve to 4–0 overall and 1–0 in SEC play. The Razorbacks, ranked 12th in the nation prior to the game, fell to 3–1.

The Crimson Tide has an all-time record of 54–21–3 (72 percent) in SEC openers dating back to the league's inception in 1933. Bama has won 20 straight SEC openers, every one since the 1992 national championship season.

The streak began with a 25–8 win over Vanderbilt on September 5, 1992. The 20-game winning streak includes 12 wins over Vanderbilt (1992-2001, 2006-07), five wins against Arkansas (2002, 2008-10) and one win against Kentucky (2003), Mississippi (2004) and South Carolina (2005). The last time Alabama lost an SEC opener was September 14, 1991, when Florida beat Alabama 35–0 in Gainesville.

The 20-game winning streak in SEC openers is the longest streak in school history and the longest active streak in the SEC. The 2011 season marked just the sixth time since divisional play began that Alabama has opened its SEC slate with a Western Division team. That also happened in 2002 (Arkansas), 2004 (Mississippi), and the last three years against (Arkansas).

Alabama leads the series with Arkansas, 12–8 (15–7 before forfeited and vacated games). Alabama and Arkansas first met on January 1, 1962, as the Tide defeated the Razorbacks, 10–3, in the Sugar Bowl en route to Alabama's sixth national championship. The Tide has won the last five meetings. Bama last lost to the Razorbacks in double overtime in Fayetteville, 24–23, on September 23, 2006.

Alabama Coach Nick Saban is 8–2 all-time against Arkansas, with his only two losses coming in his first three years at LSU in Little Rock. Saban has never lost a game to Arkansas in Baton Rouge, Fayetteville or Tuscaloosa. Saban is 5–0 against Arkansas while at the helm of the Alabama program.

Alabama has been very successful in the

The power run game served Alabama well against Arkansas, as Trent Richardson bursts through a hole for some of his 126 rushing yards.

opening month of the season under Saban. Now in his fifth season at Alabama, the Crimson Tide sports a 19–2 record in September following the win against Arkansas. Since 2008, Alabama is a perfect 16–0 in September games.

Alabama is 23–1 in its last 24 games at Bryant-Denny Stadium, dating back to the start of the 2008 season. During that stretch the Crimson Tide has been extremely stingy on defense and very effective on offense. Some of the most impressive numbers include 50 rushing touchdowns for the Alabama offense, while the Crimson Tide defense has surrendered just two rushing touchdowns at home since the beginning of the 2008 season.

Alabama has won 40 games dating back to the start of the 2008 season, which is the second-most in the Football Bowl Subdivision. The Crimson Tide won 12 games in 2008, followed that with a perfect 14–0 record in 2009 and a 10–3 mark in 2010. Alabama is one win back of Boise State, with 41 wins. The Crimson Tide has the most victories of any team that plays in a BCS conference.

Alabama led at halftime against Arkansas, 17–7. With the win, the Crimson Tide is 42–3 when leading at halftime under Saban.

Alabama was behind the Arkansas line of scrimmage much of the game as the Crimson Tide recorded ten tackles for a loss, ac-counting for 41 negative yards for the Razorbacks. Linebacker Dont'a Hightower led the way for the Alabama defense with two tackles for a loss for 8 yards and defensive tackle Jesse Williams had two tackles for a loss for 7 yards. Hightower led the Crimson Tide in tackles with a total of nine stops on the day.

Alabama held Arkansas to 17 rushing yards on 19 carries in the victory today. In the 58 games under Saban, the Crimson Tide has limited the opposition to less than 100 rushing yards 35 times, or 60 percent of the time. The 19 yards on the ground by Arkansas marks the third time this season the opposition has been held under 100 yards.

Alabama allowed just seven points in the first half of the Arkansas game. The Crimson Tide has allowed seven points or less in the first half of its last nine games. The Crimson Tide has surrendered three points or less six times over that span, including three first half shutouts.

Alabama quarterback A.J. McCarron was efficient in his first career SEC start. The redshirt sophomore was 15-of-20 for 200 yards with two touchdowns. The two touchdowns was a career best for McCarron.

Alabama found the end zone in a variety of ways on Saturday. The Crimson Tide threw for two touchdowns, rushed for one touchdown, and returned a punt and an

DeQuan Menzie pulls in his second quarter interception. He returned it for a touchdown, stretching the Alabama lead to 10. The Tide never looked back.

interception for scores. DeQuan Menzie returned an interception 25 yards for a score while Marquis Maze returned a punt 83 yards. McCarron tossed two touchdown passes, while Eddie Lacy rushed for a touchdown.

Alabama junior running back Trent Richardson scored his third touchdown on a play that was 50 yards or longer. All three scores have come in the last two games. Richardson found pay dirt on a 61-yard screen pass in the third quarter against Arkansas. He ran for two touchdowns against North Texas that were longer than 50 yards. He found the end zone on rushes of 71 and 58 yards against the Mean Green.

Richardson rushed for 126 yards on 17 carries against Arkansas on Saturday. The 126 yards on the ground marks the third straight game that Richardson has scampered over the 100-yard mark. Richardson has now recorded seven 100-yard games in his Alabama career.

Richardson has been scoring touchdowns at an impressive rate to start the 2011 season. In just four games, Richardson has found the end zone nine times. Richardson opened the year with three touchdowns against Kent State and followed that up with two more at Penn State. Richardson scored three touchdowns for Alabama against North Texas and added another against Arkansas. Richardson pushes his career total to 22 touchdowns on the ground and 28 overall. The 28 touchdowns (22 rush, 5 receiving, 1 return.) rank seventh on the Alabama career list. Shaun Alexander is the all-time leader at Alabama with 50 career touchdowns.

Alabama senior punt returner Marquis Maze took the first Crimson Tide opportunity of the second half for a touchdown on an 83-yard punt return. The punt return for a touchdown is the first of his career and the longest return of his career. The punt return was the first for a touchdown for Alabama since Javier Arenas found the end zone against Chattanooga on November. 21, 2009. The return also marked the 10th longest return for a touchdown in Alabama history.

The 1981 Alabama football team was honored in a pre-game ceremony. That Crimson Tide was a 28–17 winner over Auburn to give Coach Paul Bryant his 315th victory, making him the winningest coach in college football history.

Honorary captains from the 1981 Alabama team were former quarterback Alan Gray and former nose tackle Warren Lyles.

Captains for Alabama were tailback Trent Richardson, safety Mark Barron, linebacker Dont'a Hightower, and nose tackle Josh Chapman. ▪

C.J. Mosley tracks down an Arkansas back in the open field. The Razorbacks entered the game with one of the most-touted offenses in the country and left with their tails between their legs following a defensive masterpiece from Alabama.

Bama Throttles Florida, 38–10

A lot has been made about the prior relationship of mentor and Alabama Coach Nick Saban and student and Florida Coach Will Muschamp. Perhaps Saban forgot to tell Muschamp the fable of the tortoise and the hare.

October 1

Alabama 38

@ Florida 10

Alabama surrendered a 60-yard touchdown on the first offensive play of the game, a fast start indeed for Florida. But the Crimson Tide, not really slow, stayed steady and trounced the Gators, 38-10, in Gainesville.

Alabama improved to 5–0 on the season and 2–0 in Southeastern Conference play with the victory over 12th ranked Florida. The Gators fell to 4–1 overall and 2–1 in conference games.

A rocky start to the game was put on kilter by the Gators. It took two kickoffs to start the game (both teams committed a penalty on the first and on the re-kick Alabama kicked off out of bounds, giving the Gators the ball at the 35. Florida had a false start, and then John Brantley found Andre Debose behind Dre Kirkpatrick on a 60-yard touchdown play. Only 19 seconds had elapsed in the game, and the Gators had a 7–0 lead after Caleb Sturgis kicked the extra point.

Alabama's offense responded with a good drive, but faltered in the red zone, having to settle for a field goal. Bama marched to the Gators 14 in nine plays, Trent Richardson picking up 34 yards on five rushes and A.J. McCarron completing two passes to Michael Williams for 10 yards and one to Kenny Bell for seven yards. But then McCarron had a pass for Marquis Maze broken up—a busted play on which he got a pass to Bell in the end zone that was dropped, and overthrew Darius Hanks in the end zone.

With 9:47 to play in the first quarter, Jeremy Shelley kicked a 32-yard field goal to pull the Tide to 7–3.

Florida wasn't getting much out of the running game, but the Gators passed it down to the Tide four-yard line. After two incomplete passes, Sturgis kicked a 21-yard field goal and Florida was up by 10–3 with 5:19 to play.

A Marquis Maze runback with the ensuing kickoff went for 70 yards to the Florida 29. From there the Tide got a five-yard touchdown run from Trent Richardson, Bama having to overcome two costly red zone penalties. The big play in overcoming a holding call was an 18-yard screen to Maze to the 1. After an illegal substitution call and an incomplete pass, Richardson

With Trent Richardson and one of the toughest defenses in the country, the onus was on A.J. McCarron to be efficient in SEC play. He was solid against Florida, throwing for 140 yards and ensuring that no mistakes derailed the Crimson Tide offense.

took it in from the five and Shelley kicked it to a 10–10 tie with 52 seconds left in the first quarter.

The game was beginning to settle into a "Florida pass can't be stopped, Alabama run can't be stopped" affair, but then Bama stopped a pass. The Gators had driven to the Tide 43. Courtney Upshaw got a sack for seven yards. After a semi–busted play on which Brantley had to try a run lost a couple, Brantley tried an inside screen to Trey Burton. Upshaw stepped in front of the pass and returned it 45 yards for an Alabama touchdown. With 12:57 remaining in the second quarter, Bama had taken the lead at 17–10.

Alabama increased its lead to 24–10 with a 10-play, 61-yard drive that ended with McCarron sneaking in on a first-and-goal from the one. McCarron had completed a 16-yard third down pass to H-back Brad Smelley and a 22-yard quick screen to Richardson in the drive.

Florida had one final chance for points on a potentially costly drive. The Gators drove from the Florida 34 to the Alabama 15 with just over a minute and a half remaining in the first half. After a running play gained a yard, Brantley was sacked on consecutive plays by Alex Watkins (11 yards) and Upshaw (10 yards) the Gators had to attempt a 52-yard field goal. It missed and with five seconds remaining, the Tide was satisfied to take its two touchdown lead to the dressing room.

Waiting for his teammates in the Florida dressing room was Brantley, who had to be helped from the field and went directly to the locker room after the sack by Upshaw. Freshman Jeff Driskel took over in the second half for Florida at quarterback.

Alabama received the kickoff to start the second half, but neither Bama nor Florida could do anything with it. Each team had three punts in the third quarter, the last putting Bama back at its eight yard line with just 2:52 to play in the period.

Alabama turned that into a 92-yard touchdown drive with Richardson going the last 36 over right guard on a third-and-short situation with 12:25 remaining in the game. The 11-play march took 5:27 and gave the Crimson Tide a 31–10 lead.

Driskel fumbled a snap that was recovered by Bama's Nico Johnson at the Florida 36. It took just four plays—a couple of them Richardson out of wildcat formation—to in-

Damion Square works his way into the backfield to disrupt a play. The Gators entered the game averaging nearly 260 yards rushing per game but were only able to muster 15 against Alabama.

Trent Richardson dives for the end zone. The power running game again served Alabama well, as the Heisman candidate had a career-high 181 yards and a pair of touchdowns.

crease the Bama lead to 38–10. Back-up tailback Eddie Lacy went the last 20 yards for the touchdown with 8:45 remaining in the game and the Ben Hill Griffin Stadium exits very busy and stayed that way until the end of the game.

Alabama dominated statistically. The Tide had 21 first downs (14 rush, 6 pass, 1 penalty) to only 9 for the Gators (1 rush, 7 pass, 1 penalty).

Alabama had 226 yards rushing to 15 for the Gators. Florida had 207 yards passing on 14 of 23 completions with one interception. Bama had 12-of-25 passing for 140 yards and no interceptions.

In total offense, the Tide had 68 plays for 366 yards, an average of 5.4 yards per play. The Gators had 52 plays for 222 yards, an average of 4.3 per play.

Florida fumbled four times, losing one. Alabama did not have a fumble.

The Tide was penalized three times for 29 yards, Florida four for 20.

Alabama had nearly a 10 minute advantage in time of possession, 34:41 to 25:19.

Alabama's offensive leaders were Richardson with 29 rushes for 181 yards and two touchdowns (an average of 6.2 yards per carry) and he also had two receptions for 27 yards, a total of 208 all purpose yards. Tight end Michael Williams had three catches for 32 yards and Marquis Maze had two for 36 yards. A.J. McCarron completed 12-of-25 passes for 140 yards with no interceptions.

Cody Mandell punted five times for a 39.8 average.

Defensively, Courtney Upshaw had four tackles, including three for losses totaling 21 yards, and intercepted a pass which he returned 46 yards for a touchdown. Nico Johnson had four tackles and a fumble recovery that led to a Tide touchdown. Dont'a Hightower also had four tackles.

Florida's high-powered offense didn't deliver much after the first pass of the game. Quarterback John Brantley completed 11 of 16 passes for 190 yards, but his back-up, Jeff Driskel was good on only 2-of-6 for 14 yards. The running duo of Jeff Demps and Chris Rainey was ineffective. Demps had only three rushes for four yards, while Rainey got his four yards on 11 carries. ■

Marquis Maze left Alabama in good field position all day, averaging 41 yards per kick return. He returned one for 70 yards and chipped in on offense with a pair of catches.

McCarron Passes Tide Past Vandy

Nick Saban isn't the first Alabama football coach to have a highly-ranked Crimson Tide play down to the level of Vanderbilt. In the first half, Bama looked barely better than the second-best team in Bryant-Denny Stadium, not the No. 2 team in the nation.

October 8

Alabama 34

vs Vanderbilt 0

But all's well that ends well. Alabama finally got its game in gear with quarterback A.J. McCarron throwing four touchdown passes and went on to a 34–0 victory over Vanderbilt in the Crimson Tide's homecoming game.

Alabama improved to 6–0 overall and 3–0 in Southeastern Conference games, while the Commodores fell to 3–2 overall and 1–2 in conference games.

One problem for Bama was the Tide's short passing game was much too short. In the first half, the Tide had a handful of completed passes that actually lost yardage and several others that gained just a yard or two. In the first half, Alabama quarterback A.J. McCarron had some excellent numbers—18 of 23 for two touchdowns and no interceptions, but his 18 completions were for only 143 yards.

The rushing game was just as dismal, 14 rushes for 46 yards.

Nevertheless, Alabama managed a 14–0 first-half lead on the strength of the two McCarron touchdown passes and Vanderbilt missing on a pair of field goal opportunities.

Things picked up in the second half and Alabama finished in dominating fashion statistically. Alabama had 24 first downs, Vanderbilt 8. The Tide had 43 rushes for 153 yards, while the Commodores had 19 runs for 41 yards. Bama completed 26 of 33 passes for 266 yards with no interception; Vandy was good on 15-of-24 for 149 yards, with two interceptions.

Alabama had 76 plays for 419 yards, Vandy 43 for 190 and a time of possession advantage of 36:14 to 23:46.

Vanderbilt converted only one of 10 third down opportunities, while the Tide was good on 12 of 17.

Trent Richardson had his fifth consecutive 100-yard rushing game with 19 carries for 107 yards and Bama's lone rushing touchdown.

McCarron completed 23 of 30 passes for 237 yards and four touchdowns.

DeAndrew White goes full-extension to haul in a five-yard touchdown pass from A.J. McCarron in the second quarter. He scored a pair of touchdowns, the first of his Alabama career.

Marquis Maze had nine receptions for 93 yards, Darius Hanks five for 60, and DeAndrew White three for 58 with two touchdowns.

Mark Barron led the Tide defensively with six tackles and two pass break-ups.

It was a bit of a surprise when Vanderbilt won the toss and deferred its choice to the second half. That meant that Alabama got the football first. The Commodores short-kicked to Michael Williams so the Tide started at its own 33. It proved to be a good decision as the Tide had to punt three plays later. It was, however, just putting off what most considered to be the inevitable.

Alabama lost 16 yards on an exchange of punts, starting from its 23 on its second possession, but then marched the 77 yards in 10 plays and 3:22. Halfway through the first period, A.J. McCarron connected with Brad Smelley on a third down pass from the Vanderbilt six for the touchdown. Jeremy Shelley kicked it to 7–0.

McCarron completed passes of 12 yards and 19 yards to Darius Hanks and eight yards to DeAndrew White, and Trent Richardson ran for 20 yards to the Vanderbilt 13 to set up the touchdown.

Vanderbilt had a nice drive into Alabama territory, but on a third and inches from inside the Tide 27, Commodores quarterback Larry Smith was stuffed by Tide nose tackle Josh Chapman on a quarterback draw. That forced a 47-yard field goal attempt of 47 yards by Carey Spear. It was just short, hitting the cross bar and bouncing back, no good, with 3:11 left in the first quarter.

Smith appeared to be injured on the draw and on subsequent Vandy offensive series the quarterback was Jordan Rodgers. Rodgers directed a nice drive into Alabama territory, but the Commodores had to settle for another field goal attempt. This one from 38 yards was wide right.

Alabama closed out first half scoring with only 21 seconds remaining until intermission. McCarron did a nice job of directing a 13-play, 78-yard drive that took 3:57. The Tide march got bailed out by an early pass interference call against the Commodores that gave Bama the ball at midfield.

McCarron hit Marquis Maze on a 29-yard gain to the Vanderbilt 25 with 54 seconds remaining in the half. Back-to-back completions to Smelley got it to the 12 and a completion to Maze put it at the five with 32 seconds to play. McCarron was under pressure and overthrew an open Hanks in the end zone, but made up for it on third-and-three.

It appeared McCarron could have scrambled into the end zone,

Dee Milliner steps in front of a pass from Vanderbilt backup Jordan Rodgers. It was tough day at the office for the Commodore signal callers, with NFL star Aaron Rodgers' younger brother throwing a pair of interceptions in relief of the injured Larry Smith.

but he passed to DeAndrew White at the back of the end zone for the touchdown. Shelley's kick made it 14–0 at intermission.

McCarron directed an excellent drive on Bama's first second half possession, although the quarterback attempted and completed only one pass in the march. After a block-in-the-back penalty wiped out a nice Maze punt return and started Alabama at its own 6, the Tide went 94 yards in 12 plays.

Trent Richardson started the drive with three runs that gave Bama some breathing room. Moments later Richardson stacked nice runs, a 19-yarder and a 24-yarder, to push the Tide to the Vandy 26. Jalston Fowler took over at tailback and in a couple of carries had it inside the five. Richardson returned to tailback and run it in with 6:03 left in the third quarter.

Alabama began to stretch it out late in the third quarter, although an impressive touchdown had the ignominy of Shelley's first missed extra point of the season.

The third touchdown pass of the night for McCarron was a 39-yard, third-down pass to DeAndrew White, who split a couple of Vandy defenders and made a fine catch. The Tide had a 27–0 lead after Shelley's missed PAT.

McCarron had a 19-yard gain on a short pass to Maze to get it moving, Richardson ran for 10, and McCarron completed a 12-yard pass to Brandon Gibson before the scoring pass.

McCarron got his fourth touchdown pass of the night following a nice interception and return by Dee Milliner. Milliner picked Rodgers at the Tide 43 and ran it down to the Vandy 20. On a third-down play, Darius Hanks got open in the end zone and McCarron hit him for the touchdown. Shelley kicked it to 34–0 with 12:16 remaining in the game.

Nico Johnson gave the Tide an opportunity for another score when the Bama linebacker turned in an interception at the Vanderbilt 37 with about 10 minutes to play. Alabama substitutes, including Phillip Sims at quarterback, took over and the Tide was unable to get into scoring position before turning the ball over to the Commodores.

After a shanked Vandy punt, the Tide kept the ball until almost the end, again coming up short in Commodores territory. ■

Plenty of room up the middle for Trent Richardson as he picks up more yards in his fifth straight 100-yard game. He scored from a yard out in the third quarter to make it 21–0.

Alabama Brutalizes Ole Miss, 52–7

Get your hotty toddy while you can. For Mississippi, the pleasure was short, the pain intense. The Rebels got off to a quick lead hosting Alabama in Oxford Saturday evening, but the Crimson Tide rolled as expected.

October 15

Alabama 52

@ Ole Miss 7

Trent Richardson scored four touchdowns and Alabama scored the final 52 points of the game in downing Ole Miss, 52–7.

Second-ranked Bama ran its record to 7–0, including a 4–0 record in Southeastern Conference games. The Rebels fell to 2–4 overall, 0–3 in the conference.

Asked how good Alabama could be if it played for 60 minutes, Tide Coach Nick Saban said, "I thought we did, but I guess you can't count those 30 seconds at the start of the game." As had been the case in a big road game at Florida a few weeks ago, the Rebels got a big play and had an early lead on a 72-yard drive. Those 72 yards would be more than half the game total for the home team against the Alabama defense.

As would be expected, Alabama had a huge advantage statistically.

The Tide had 27 first downs, Ole Miss nine. Bama rushed 42 times for 389 yards (9.3 yards per rush), the Rebels 31 carries for 28 yards, less than one yard per rush. Alabama quarterbacks completed 20 of 25 passes for 226 yards with no interceptions. Mississippi completed 10 of 21 passes passes with one interception for 113 yards.

Alabama's total offense was 615 yards on 67 plays, 9.2 yards per play. Ole Miss had 52 plays for 141 yards, 2.7 yards per play.

Alabama punted one time for 44 yards, the Rebels seven times for 278 yards.

Bama did not fumble. Ole Miss fumbled once and the Tide recovered it, and it led to a Bama touchdown.

Richardson rushed 17 times for 183 yards and four touchdowns. He had a long run of 76 yards. Jalston Fowler had nine carries for 125 yards and two touchdowns. Blake Sims came in late and had five rushes for 74 yards.

Quarterback A.J. McCarron completed 19 of 24 passes for 224 yards and one touchdown.

Darius Hanks had four receptions for 63 yards.

Ole Miss struck quickly as wide receiver Nickolas Brassell was wide open behind Tide cornerback Dee Milliner for a 59-yard gain to

With Chance Warmack out in front of him, Trent Richardson hits the outside on his seven-yard second-quarter touchdown run that gave the Crimson Tide a 14–7 lead. It was a career day for the running back, who ran for 183 yards and four touchdowns, the last a 76-yard effort that gave Richardson his Heisman moment.

the Bama 2. Two plays later Jeff Scott went in untouched on a right end toss sweep. Bryson Rose kicked the Rebels to a 7–0 lead. The five-play drive covered 72 yards and took just over two minutes.

It took Alabama barely four minutes to tie the score with Trent Richardson sweeping left end for an eight-yard touchdown run and Jeremy Shelley kicking it to 7–7 with 8:24 left in the first quarter. Bama went 79 yards in nine plays, including a couple of nifty third-down conversions. Facing third-and-two at the Bama 29, almost veryone expected Richardson to get the ball, but A.J. McCarron hit tight end Michael Williams on a crossing pattern that went for 34 yards to the Ole Miss 37. From the 27 on third-and-10, McCarron connected with wide receiver DeAndrew White on a crossing route for 15 to the 12. Two Richardson runs finished off the drive.

Alabama took the lead on Richardson's second touchdown run on the second play of the second quarter. His seven-yard run capped a 10-play, 62-yard drive. Prior to the touchdown, Richardson had two 11-yard runs and also had a 10-yard run from wildcat on a fourth-and-two situation at the Rebels' 31. Prior to the touchdown run, McCarron ran on a designed play from empty backfield and gained four yards. With 14:11 remaining in the second quarter, Shelley kicked it to Alabama 14, Mississippi 7.

The first flag of the game hurt Alabama's scoring chances after the Tide started at its 20 following an Ole Miss punt. McCarron completed passes of seven yards to Marquis Maze, five to Williams, and six to Brad Smelley around a 15-yard run by Eddie Lacy. But on a first-and-10 from the Ole Miss 42, Lacy's long run was wiped out by a holding call and the Tide couldn't overcome it. On fourth-and-four from the Ole Miss 36, Cade Foster's 53-yard field goal attempt was short.

The Rebels elected to return the kick and Foster was injured on the runback.

The second and third penalties of the game against Alabama may have turned a touchdown into a field goal. Robert Lester, the leader in interceptions in the SEC last year with eight, made his first of the year at the Alabama 39 and returned it almost to the end zone. However, a block in the back penalty forced Alabama to start at the Ole Miss 41.

Bama moved to the Ole Miss 13, and from there Richardson took it in for what appeared to be his third touchdown of the game, but a holding call on center William Vlachos —he had also been flagged on the previous series—pushed the Tide back. Eventually, Richardson had a 15-yard gain for a third-and-three at the Rebels' three-yard line, but a third down pass was incomplete. Alabama settled for a 24-yard Shelley field goal and a 17–7 halftime lead.

Richardson got that third touchdown on the first series of the second half. Alabama went 73 yards in six plays after taking the kickoff. McCarron completed a 10-yard pass to Marquis Maze on a third-down play, then passed to Richardson for 15 and Darius Hanks for 36 to the Rebs' 8. On first and goal, Richardson took it in and Shelley kicked it to 24–7. The drive had taken 2:23, which was forever compared to the next one.

After an Ole Miss punt went out of bounds at the Alabama 8, the Tide used two Richardson runs to cover the 92 yards. The tailback went over right guard for 16. From the 24, Richardson took the ball going left, broke through and up the middle, and then down the right sidelines. He seemed to be hemmed in as he approached the 10-yard line, but made a move and went in for his fourth touchdown. The "drive" had taken 48 seconds. Shelley kicked it to 31–7.

The next touchdown drive would be even quicker, 41

Robert Lester intercepts Randall Mackey and returns it inside the five-yard line. Though most of the return was negated by penalty, it was a highlight for the crushing Alabama defense.

seconds. Ole Miss quarterback Mackey was hit on a sack by Courtney Upshaw, who had not played in the first quarter of the game. The ball popped out and Ed Stinson recovered for Bama at the Mississippi 15. Bama's third tailback, Jalston Fowler, made two runs, one for seven yards, the second for eight and the touchdown. Shelley kicked it to 38–7 with 6:44 remaining in the third quarter.

A mass exit had begun from Vaught-Hemingway Stadium. The original crowd had been the fourth largest in stadium history, 61,792.

The third quarter onslaught continued after Bama's kick-off coverage held the Rebels at the 14 and the Tide defense—led by Upshaw's sack for an eight-yard loss—put the Rebels in a deep hole to punt.

After taking over at the 41, McCarron completed a 17-yard pass to Kenny Bell. Three Fowler runs got it to the Rebels 10. McCarron then hit Brandon Gibson for the touchdown. The 41-yard drive had taken 2:17 and five plays. Shelley kicked it to 45–7, which is how the third quarter ended.

It continued into the fourth quarter. A goal-line stand by Alabama, holding the Rebels to zero yards on four runs from the Crimson Tide two-yard line, put Bama in a hole. The second offense with Phillip Sims at quarterback took over. Jalston Fowler got Bama out of the hole. He ran for two yards, and then for 22 to the Alabama 26. After a couple of short gains, on third-and-five Fowler got the ball going over right guard, burst through the Mississippi defense, and went 69 yards for the touchdown. With 10:08 to play, Shelley kicked it to 52–7. The five-play, 92-yard drive took 2:44.

Although over 10 minutes remained, Bama second teamers mercifully did not attempt to run it up. ■

Safety Robert Lester looks for running room after intercepting Ole Miss quarterback Randall Mackey in the second quarter. The Crimson Tide forced a pair of turnovers and allowed the Rebels just 113 yards of total offense.

National Awards To Richardson, Jones

Alabama players won two of the nation's top individual awards on the Disney Boardwalk near Orlando. The Crimson Tide produced its first Doak Walker Award and third winner of the Outland Trophy.

Alabama junior running back Trent Richardson became the first Tide player to win the Doak Walker Award as the nation's best running back and junior offensive tackle Barrett Jones became the third Bama player to win the Outland Trophy as the finest interior lineman in the nation.

The awards were presented as part of the Home Depot College Football Awards Show held at the Atlantic Dance Hall on the Disney Boardwalk.

Richardson and Jones were also part of the large contingent of Alabama players who were named to the Walter Camp All-America team. They were joined on the first team by linebacker Dont'a Hightower and safety Mark Barron. Center William Vlachos and linebacker Courtney Upshaw were second team selections.

Richardson, a native of Pensacola, Florida, has also been named the Southeastern Conference Offensive Player of the Year and a SEC first-team honoree. He also earned first team AFCA All-American honors. He will be in New York later this week as one of the five finalists for the Heisman Trophy as the nation's most outstanding player.

The powerful back is fifth in the nation in rushing yards per game, averaging 131.92, and has scored 23 touchdowns this season, ranking him fifth in scoring at 11.5 points per game. This season, Richardson set the Alabama record for rushing touchdowns in a season with 20. That ties him for second most in a season in SEC history.

Jones, a native of Germantown, Tennessee, anchors the Alabama offensive line from his left tackle position. He has started 35 career games, including 10 at left tackle in 2011. He has also helped the Tide rank 15th nationally and first in the SEC in rushing (219.83), while blocking for the league's No. 2 scoring offense at 36.0 points per game.

Jones has also been named an AFCA All-American on top of earning All-SEC first team. Off the field, Jones has been recognized as the Wuerfell Trophy winner along with the SEC Scholar-Athlete of the Year.

Jones joins former Crimson Tide offensive linemen and National Football League first round picks Chris Samuels (1999) and Andre Smith (2008) as Outland Trophy winners. ■

Trent Richardson was the nation's finest tailback in one of the country's most bruising offenses. He took home the Doak Walker Award and finished third in Heisman voting.

With one of the best offensive lines ever assembled, Richardson nearly always had big holes to rumble through.

Alabama Explodes To Rout Vols, 37–6

That sound you heard in the first half at Bryant-Denny Stadium— ZZZZZZ—wasn't really Alabama sleepwalking. It was the burning fuse that ignited a second-half explosion and carried the Crimson Tide to a convincing 37–6 victory over Tennessee Saturday night.

October 22

Alabama 37

vs Tennessee 6

Alabama Coach Nick Saban can blame whomever he wishes for his Crimson Tide football team not being ready to play when the game started. If it's because of a focus on LSU, that really is a bad excuse because if the Tide plays against the Bengal Tigers the way it did against Tennessee to open the game, Bama will be road kill.

On the other hand, there was a good reason fans began chanting for LSU late in the third quarter. The attention could officially turn to what is being billed as one of the great regular season games of all-time.

Both Alabama and LSU did what they had to do on Saturday and through the first eight games of 2011. LSU, ranked first in the nation, blasted Auburn, 45–10, while the second-ranked Tide was taking care of Tennessee.

Alabama is now 8–0 overall and 5–0 in Southeastern Conference games. Tennessee fell to 3–4 overall and 0–4 in league games.

After a lethargic first half in which both

Bama and the Vols kicked a pair of field goals, Alabama's third quarter included 12 first-down plays that netted 178 yards and two touchdowns. The other touchdown came on a second-down play. There were no third-down or fourth-down Bama plays in the quarter, which ended with Alabama holding a 27–6 lead going to the fourth quarter.

The third-quarter domination included Alabama having nine first downs, Tennessee zero. The Tide had 14 plays for 190 yards. Tennessee's third quarter was 13 plays for 31 yards. Quarterback A.J. McCarron passed seven times in the third quarter, completing all seven for 125 yards.

For the game, McCarron completed 17 of 26 passes for 284 yards and a touchdown. He suffered one interception and was sacked once, on the final play of the first half. His touchdown pass was 39 yards to Kenny Bell in the third quarter. McCarron also ran for a touchdown in the third quarter.

Tailback Trent Richardson had his streak of

Still protecting the ball, Trent Richardson high-steps into the end zone for one of his two second-half touchdowns. After the game started slow and was tied at halftime, Alabama turned up the heat in a 31–0 second-half run.

100-yard rushing games end with 17 carries for 77 yards. He did have two rushing touchdowns.

The rest of the scoring came from placekickers Jeremy Shelley and Cade Foster. Shelley made two first-half field goals and four extra-point kicks and Foster was good on a 45-yard fourth-quarter field goal.

Marquis Maze had five receptions for 106 yards.

Linebacker C.J. Mosley was in on eight tackles. Dont'a Hightower was in on seven tackles, including a sack and a tackle for loss, and also had an interception. Courtney Upshaw and Chris Jordan caused fumbles and Vinnie Sunseri had a fumble recovery.

Tennessee Coach Derek Dooley had a cute one-liner early in the week when he suggested it was bad policy to score first against Alabama because it irritated the Crimson Tide. Florida and Ole Miss had both scored first against Bama and then suffered beat down losses at the hands of the Tide.

But the Vols had no choice. Alabama opened the game not hitting on all cylinders, offensively or defensively, and Tennessee drove deep into Bama territory late in the first quarter. The Vols completed a 12-play drive to a 40-yard field goal by Mike Palardy and a 3–0 Tennessee lead.

Bama had at least two chances to stop the march, which included two penalties against the Vols. On a fourth-and-3, the Vols went for it, completing a pass that was short of the first down. However, the receiver got out of the grasp of Bama cornerback DeQuan Menzie and went for an 11-yard gain to the Tide 24. Two plays later a pass in the end zone went through the hands of Alabama safety Mark Barron. Although the drive covered only 45 yards, it took 12 plays and consumed 6:37.

Alabama was able to tie the score moments later, but it was a disheartening field goal. On first down following a kickoff, Tide quarterback A.J. McCarron completed that elusive downfield pass, hitting Marquis Maze down the left sideline. Maze took it for a 69-yard gain to the Tennessee 12.

From there Bama tried one Trent Richardson run, then twice McCarron had to scramble before throwing the ball away. Jeremy Shelley came on to kick a 26-yard field goal and tie the score at 3–3 with 2:26 left in the first quarter.

Alabama took a 6–3 lead after another drive deep into Tennessee territory. After a poor Tennessee punt that gave Bama the ball at its 40, McCarron completed a 21-yard pass to Darius Hanks to the Vols 39. Back-to-back passes to Eddie Lacy, a five-yarder on the last play of the first quarter and a nine-yard gain on the first play of the second quarter, moved to the Tennessee 25. McCarron then found Richardson on a safety valve and he bulled for 10 yards to a first down at Tennessee's 12. A first down pass was just out of the reach of tight end Mike Williams in the end zone, and two plays later Shelley had to kick a 29-yard field goal. With 10:55 remaining Bama had the lead at 6–3.

Tennessee scored the first second quarter points against Alabama this season to tie the game at 6–6. Poor Alabama defense was a contributing factor. The Vols were in the shadow of their goal line after a holding call made it first-and-20 at the Tennessee 10, but Poole got away on a 13-yard run. After the Volunteers were flagged for five more yards in penalties, quarterback Matt Simms connected with wide receiver Da'Rick Rogers on a 21-yard gain. Still, it seemed Alabama had stopped the drive. On fourth-and-four from the Tennessee 47, however, punter Palardy passed complete to wide receiver Anthony Anderson for five yards. Bama added to the bad with a face-mask penalty on the play, putting the Vols at the Tide 33. Although Bama's defense got the drive stopped there, Palardy kicked a 52-yard field goal with 5:03 to tie the score at 6–6, which would be the halftime score.

It was a completely different Alabama that returned from intermission.

First Bama stopped the Vols, three and out. And then McCarron began slinging. He found Richardson on a safety

Richardson falls forward for extra yards as a Tennessee tackler wraps him up. After finishing with 77 yards rushing, Richardson was left tied with Shaun Alexander for the most consecutive 100-yard running games in school history with six.

valve, and Richardson turned it into a 22-yard gain. Then he completed passes to Darius Hanks (14), Maze (20) and Brad Smelley for 17 and a first-and-goal at the Tennessee two. On first down McCarron kept at right end, diving in with the ball inside the pylon to make it 13–6.

Tennessee made an ill-advised decision to go for it on fourth-and-inches at the Tennessee 39. When Simms was stacked up by Josh Chapman and Hightower for no gain, McCarron made quick work of the opportunity. He connected down the middle with Kenny Bell in the end zone for a one-play, nine-second "drive." It was 20–6.

After the Bama defense held the Vols on another three-and-out, McCarron took the Tide on a six-play, 63-yard drive that took 3:15. McCarron completed a 12-yard pass to Maze, then turned it over to the infantry. Eddie Lacy had runs of 13 and 19 yards and then Richardson took it for 16 to the Tennessee 3.

A holding call put it back at the 13, and two plays later Richardson took it 12 yards up the middle, emerging from under a pile of humanity into the end zone. It was near the end of the third quarter and the issue was pretty much decided with Alabama in control, 27–6.

Over the last minute of the third quarter and the first three minutes of the fourth quarter, the Tide drove the ball from its 27 to the Tennessee 27, but had to settle for a 45-yard Foster field goal and a 30–6 lead.

The defense set up the final score. Nico Johnston tipped a Matt Simms pass, which was picked off by Hightower at the Tennessee 38 and returned to the nine. Three runs by Richardson got the final score with 9:27 remaining. It was 37–6 and Alabama could ease off the accelerator.

A late fumble recovery by freshman safety Vinnie Sunseri in Tennessee territory resulted in the rest of the game being played on the Vols' side of the field. Jalston Fowler came up inches short of another touchdown, and then Bama ran out the game with back-up quarterback Phillip Sims taking a knee. ■

Marquis Maze caught five passes for 106 yards against Tennessee, including a 69-yard reception in the first quarter that set up a game-tying Alabama field goal.

LSU Wins Defensive Struggle In OT

One would have thought Les Miles was coaching Alabama, except the goofball play didn't work. It backfired, and Alabama lost the biggest regular season game in its history, and probably any chance at any kind of championship in a year that had been so full of promise.

November 5

Alabama 6 (OT)

vs LSU 9

It was Alabama Coach Nick Saban who decided to be tricky in the fourth quarter of a tie game. Instead of getting points, the Crimson Tide ended up in overtime. LSU solidified its No. 1 national ranking with a 9–6 overtime victory over Bama at Bryant-Denny Stadium.

Drew Alleman was good on his third field goal of the night from 25 yards to end the game in the initial overtime period.

Alabama attempted six field goals, making two and having one blocked. The final miss, an unlikely 52-yard effort by Cade Foster in overtime, came after Alabama—going on offense first in the extra football—managed to travel backwards via penalty and sack.

LSU took its opportunity to run the ball to inside the 10-yard line and knock through the chip shot winner.

It was the only time in the game that LSU had the lead.

LSU improved to 9–0 overall and 6–0 in Southeastern Conference games. Alabama, which had been ranked second in the nation going into the game, fell to 8–1 and 5–1.

Both teams made one field goal in each half.

Alabama had numerous missed opportunities in the first half, and not just because the Tide was 0-for-3 on field goals before making one.

Alabama had a first down at the LSU 30 on Bama's first possession and ended with Cade Foster trying a 44-yard field goal which was wide right. On the Tide's second possession a first down at the LSU earned no more than a 50-yard field goal try by Foster, also wide right.

Late in the first quarter Bama safety Robert Lester intercepted a Jarrett Lee pass at the Alabama 47. A low snap that was briefly fumbled may have contributed to the interception. But Bama couldn't convert. After driving to a first down at the LSU 24, Alabama faced a fourth-and-17. The Tide didn't give up on a possible field goal, calling

Nick Saban watches on as his current team battles his old in one of the titanic struggles of the college football season. It was a frustrating game to watch for Saban, as his kickers combined to miss four field goals.

on Jeremy Shelley for a 49-yard try. The third time was not the charm for Alabama as the kick was blocked.

Later in the quarter a fine LSU punt pinned Bama at its four. A Trent Richardson run of 12 yards got the ball out of the shadow of the goal line. A 15-yard face mask penalty against LSU on a short Richardson run helped the cause. And then quarterback A.J. McCarron hit Richardson on a short pass. Richardson made two defenders miss as he turned the play into a 39-yard gain to the LSU 19. Again the drive stalled, but this time Shelley was able to make a 34-yard field goal and give the Tide a 3–0 lead with 3:53 to play.

That 3:53 proved to be just enough time for LSU to tie the score. With Jordan Jefferson at quarterback and Michael Ford at tailback, the Tigers drove to a first-and-goal at the Alabama 8 on the strength of a 34-yard pass from Jefferson to Russell Shepard. Helped by a holding call against Alabama, LSU threatened to score a touchdown, but had to settle for a last-play-of-the-half Drew Alleman 19-yard field goal.

After 30 minutes of play, it was Alabama 3, LSU 3.

Alabama got two early breaks in the third quarter and managed to get only three points. The first was a 22-yard LSU punt that set the Tide up at midfield. But after no movement, Cody Mandell was called on for the first Alabama punt of the night. He put it out of bounds at the LSU 17.

Jarrett Lee hadn't been seen at quarterback in a while, but returned to action—and promptly threw an interception. Alabama safety Mark Barron picked it off and appeared to have returned the ball to inside the LSU five-yard line. A block in the back, however, put the Tide back to the LSU 35.

McCarron went to Kenny Bell, trying for the quick score, but was incomplete. After a short Richardson run and a dump pass to Marquis Maze put Bama at the 29, the Tide called on Foster for a 46-yard field goal try and Foster made it for a 6–3 lead with 7:56 remaining in the third quarter.

Later in the quarter, Alabama had moved from its 11 to its 41, but a McCarron pass intended for Brad Smelley was intercepted by LSU cornerback Morris Claiborne at the Tide 48 and returned to the Tide 15. Although the Bama defense was stiff, the Tigers got a 30-yard Alleman field goal in the opening minute of the fourth quarter. It was 6–6.

Alabama got two great efforts that might have resulted in

A.J. McCarron had a fine day against one of the country's best defenses, completing 16 of 28 passes for 199 yards. He had an unfortunate interception in the second half, however, that set up LSU's game-tying field goal.

Alabama's defense remained stout in the face of LSU's potent offense.

winning points. A short pass to Marquis Maze was turned into an 18-yard run on a third-down play. Two plays later, a short pass to Richardson was turned into a nifty 24-yard gain to the LSU 28.

As had been the case too many times, Alabama did not take advantage of being deep in LSU territory. In the fourth quarter of a tie game in which there had been only four field goals, points were at a premium.

Alabama decided to try a trick play for a touchdown. It almost worked. Instead, it killed the opportunity. Marquis Maze was in wildcat formation and tried a long pass to tight end Michael Williams. Williams got the ball at the one, but on the way to the ground had it stripped away by LSU's Eric Reid. The Tigers had the ball at their one.

Although Bama would force a punt, Maze let it go and it rolled for 73 yards to the Alabama 19. The Tide ground out a couple of first downs, but then went in a hole and ended up with a fourth and two near midfield and had to punt the ball away. The Tide would not get it back until only 52 seconds remained and Alabama opted to play for the win in overtime.

As is often the case, the team that wins the coin toss wins the game. LSU won the toss and elected to go on defense.

It was a terrible offensive performance by Alabama. A hurried pass on an inside screen to Richardson was incomplete and then the Tide was flagged for an illegal substitution penalty. A wheel route to Richardson looked like it might score a touchdown, but the pass went just off Richardson's hands, incomplete. On third down McCarron took a sack, a five-yard loss that pushed the field goal try back to 52 yards. It wasn't close.

LSU got its chance and the Tigers knew they needed only a field goal to win. A run by Ware gained three and then on an option, Ford got 15 to the seven. From there the Tigers maneuvered into position for Alleman's game-winning kick.

Alabama had 60 plays for 295 yards to LSU's 58 plays for 239 yards in the defensive struggle. Richardson was held under 100 yards rushing as he had 23 carries for a net of 89 yards. McCarron completed 16 of 28 passes for 199 yards with one interception. Maze had six catches for 61 yards, Richardson five for 80. Nico Johnson led the Tide defensively with 11 tackles, followed by DeQuan Menzie with eight and Dont'a Hightower with seven. Courtney Upshaw had six tackles, a sack, and two quarterback pressures. ■

Trent Richardson finds some running room down the sideline. It was a bruising day for the Alabama back, as he carried 23 times for 89 yards against a stout LSU defense.

Bama Bounces Back, Beating Bulldogs

Alabama appeared to be suffering a bit of a hangover from last week's loss to LSU, but the Crimson Tide was very good on defense and just good enough on offense to overcome some not-so-special kicking game work and pick up a Southeastern Conference victory on the road.

November 12

Alabama 24

@ Mississippi State 7

Alabama went into Starkville and defeated the Mississippi State Bulldogs, 24–7. With the win, Alabama improved to 9–1 overall and 6–1 in Southeastern Conference games. The Crimson Tide went into the contest ranked fourth in the nation in the polls and third in the BCS standings. Unranked Mississippi State fell to 5–5 overall and 1–5 in SEC games.

Eddie Lacy scored two touchdowns, including a 32-yard run in the final moments of the game when Bama was trying to run out the clock. While that may have made the final margin deceptively wide, the domination by the Tide was total.

Alabama never trailed in the game as the Crimson Tide had 20 first downs to only nine for Mississippi State. Bama's best-in-the-nation defense was able to hold the Bulldogs to 12 yards on 29 carries, an average of about a foot per carry. Meanwhile, Alabama had 44 rushes

for 223 yards, an average of 5.1 yards per rush.

In passing, Bama was good on 14 of 24 passes with one interception for 163 yards, while holding the Dogs to 15-of-30 for 119 yards. Alabama defenders turned in five sacks, Mississippi State none.

Alabama had total offense of 68 plays for 368 yards (5.7 per play), the Bulldogs 59 plays for 131 yards (2.2 per play).

Alabama was led in rushing by Trent Richardson, who had 22 carries for 127 yards and one touchdown, but in half as many carries, Eddie Lacy had 96 yards and two touchdowns.

Kevin Norwood was the big-play man—and something of a surprise big-play man—in the receiving game with two catches for 60 yards.

Dont'a Hightower had another big game on defense with four primary tackles and seven assists and also had 1.5 sacks for nine yards and 2.5 tackles for loss for 10 yards and broke up one

Once again his explosive self, Trent Richardson barrels into the open field on a 25-yard run in the fourth quarter. He carried in from two yards out two plays later, the jewel of his 127-yard day.

pass. Although the official statistics did not credit him with a quarterback pressure, he definitely was in the face of the Bulldogs quarterbacks.

Mark Barron was in on nine tackles and C.J. Mosley was in on seven tackles.

Alabama had only a 7–0 lead at halftime as Crimson Tide field goal kickers missed two tries, including a relatively short 31-yard attempt (an extra point kick is equivalent to a 19-yard field goal). But thanks to the Bama defense and Mississippi State also missing two field goals—including a 29-yard try after the Bulldogs started with a first and goal at the Tide 4—Alabama carried a shutout into the intermission.

Alabama got on the scoreboard with a five-play, 52-yard drive that benefitted from two big Mississippi State penalties. Bama punt return man Marquis Maze took a State punt at the Tide 33 and ran out of bounds, where he was tackled. The personal foul penalty gave Bama the start at its 48.

Mississippi native Kevin Norwood, who has not been used much as a receiver, caught a 21-yard pass to get the march started. Trent Richardson kept it going with a 15-yard run, but then went out of the game.

Eddie Lacy ran for six and then Bama had a false start. After another short run, Mississippi State was flagged for pass interference at the Bulldogs 3. Lacy went left end and dived into the end zone for the touchdown with 9:59 to play in the second quarter. Jeremy Shelley kicked the extra point —twice. The touchdown was reviewed after he kicked the first extra point, but he was good on the second try, too.

Alabama had missed field goals in the first quarter (Cade Foster on a 49-yard try) and earlier in the second quarter (Shelley on a 31-yard try).

Just before halftime, the Mississippi State defense made a play that threatened to tie the game, or at least get points for the Bulldogs. Linebacker Carson Lawrence picked off a McCarron pass at the 35 and returned it to the Alabama 4, where it was first-and-goal with 2:15 until intermission. State had two pass incompletions around a run for a three-yard loss and a false start penalty, and faced fourth-and-goal from the 12. Brian Egan missed the three-point try and the Tide had a 7–0 halftime lead.

Earlier in the quarter State's Derek DePasquale had missed on a 41-yard field goal try.

Alabama got points on its first possession of the second half, but not the points the Tide wanted. After a Mississippi State punt to the end zone, the Tide moved quickly into State territory with a 38-yard pass from McCarron to Norwood. McCarron then hit DeAndrew White on an eight=yard pass and Trent Richardson ran for six. After a penalty against the Tide for an ineligible receiver, Richardson ran 20 yards for a first down at the Bulldogs 13. When Richardson got eight yards on first down, a Bama touchdown seemed likely, but the next two plays lost a couple of yards and Bama settled for a 24-yard Shelley field goal and a 10–0 lead.

Remaining highlights of the third quarter were a couple of ill-advised gambles. On a fourth-and-inches at midfield, a McCarron quarterback sneak failed to gain. A few minutes later State tried a pass on fourth-and-seven that fell incomplete.

Alabama took advantage of its good field position. On

Vick Ballard rumbles right into the Alabama defensive line. He had nearly 1200 yards on the season, but was game for just 21 yards against an angry Crimson Tide.

first down, McCarron hit Marquis Maze for 13 yards and a first down to the State 40 and three more plays before the end of the third quarter got a first down at the Bulldogs 28.

On the first play of the fourth quarter, Richardson streaked around right end for a 24-yard gain, barely stepping out of bounds at the four. It took the junior tailback two carries to put it in the end zone. With Shelley's PAT kick, Bama had a 17–0 lead.

Alabama's kickoffs continue to be sub-par. Foster's kickoff carried only to the MSU 10 and was returned 68 yards to the Alabama 22. This time the defense couldn't hold. Tyler Russell ran for 14 yards to the eight. After a penalty put the ball back at the 12, second-and-goal, Russell connected with Chris Smith at the goalline and he went in for the touchdown with just over 12 minutes to play. DePasquale's PAT made it Alabama 17, Mississippi State 7.

After Alabama was forced to punt on its next possession, the Bulldogs started at their 20 and had some success. A fourth-and-inches gamble from the 29 was good. But after a sack by Josh Chapman and two incomplete passes, State had to punt the ball away.

Alabama started at its 27 and with 6:26 to play seemed to have its only goal being to run time. It was very successful. After a false start, Trent Richardson ran the ball nine consecutive times for a total of 43 yards and three first downs. He also burned five minutes of clock time.

Lacy came on in relief and ran three yards. After State used its last timeout, Lacy delivered the insult to injury, going around left end untouched for a 32-yard touchdowns that came with just 1:18 to play. ■

Eddie Lacy finds himself off his feet in the Mississippi State secondary. Hobbled by injury in recent weeks, the resurgent Lacy ripped off 96 yards and a pair of touchdowns.

Tide Has Enough To Down Eagles

Alabama had enough offensive punch to overcome Georgia Southern's effective offense and special teams play that resulted in quick scores against the Crimson Tide. But it's not fastest that counts. It's most.

November 19

Alabama 45

vs Georgia Southern 21

Alabama didn't always look great in doing it, but the Crimson Tide was a 45–21 winner over Georgia Southern at Bryant-Denny Stadium. The Crimson Tide improved to 10–1 overall while the Eagles fell to 9–2.

Alabama was ranked third in the nation going into the game with the prospect of moving to No. 2 in the nation following Oklahoma State's loss to unranked Iowa State Friday night.

Alabama followers enjoyed watching the wishbone through the 1970s and early 1980s when Coach Paul Bryant's Bama teams were racking up yards and wins and championships. It's not so much fun from the other side. Major college teams rarely see true option offense teams.

That explains why the Eagles were able to get the most points any opponent has scored on Alabama this year. Georgia Southern also rushed 39 times for 302 yards with fullback Dominique Swope having 18 carries for 153 yards, including an 82-yard touchdown run.

But Alabama was able to more than match the Eagles in offense. Bama had 49 rushes for 272 yards and quarterback A.J. McCarron completed 14 of 19 passes for 190 yards and three touchdowns.

Trent Richardson had 32 carries for 175 yards and two touchdowns and also had a touchdown reception. Brad Smelley had two touchdown receptions as he caught four passes for 58 yards. Brand Gibson caught four passes for 49 yards and Marquis Maze had three receptions for 44 yards.

Mark Barron led Bama with eight primary tackles. Quinton Dial had three primary stops and five assists. Nico Johnson and Dont'a Hightower were in on six each and Hightower had a blocked field goal attempt that resulted in an Alabama touchdown.

Alabama was not sharp to open the game. The Tide's first drive went well enough for three plays—two complete passes from A.J. McCarron to Brandon Gibson for 24 yards around a

Adding 175 yards to his Heisman résumé, Trent Richardson is seen here leaping over the line for a second-quarter touchdown, the second of his three scores."

12-yard run by Trent Richardson—but then bogged down inside the Georgia Southern 20. Jeremy Shelley kicked the Tide to a 3–0 lead with a 32-yard field goal less than four minutes into the game.

The Georgia Southern triple option would give Alabama's defense problems from the start. The Eagles moved from their 26 to the Alabama 23 in four plays before Damion Square and Quinton Dial caught Georgia Southern quarterback Jabo Shaw for consecutive losses, forcing a field goal try from the Alabama 25.

Adrian Mora's 42-yard effort was blocked by Tide linebacker Dont'a Hightower and picked up at the Georgia Southern 45 by Bama cornerback Dre Kirkpatrick, who returned it 55 yards for a touchdown. With 5:12 to play in the first quarter, Alabama had a 10–0 lead.

It looked as though Alabama was taking charge of the game when the Tide forced the Eagles to punt and started a drive at the Alabama 29.

Richardson had back-to-back runs of 15 and 12 yards. Eddie Lacy gave Richardson a breather and Lacy took an outlet pass from McCarron for 13. Bama had to overcome a block-in-the-back penalty with Lacy running for 19 and seven on back-to-back plays for a first down at the Georgia Southern 15 as the first quarter ended. Four plays later Richardson took a short pass from McCarron for a four-yard touchdown and the Tide had a 17–0 lead.

That margin didn't last long.

After Cade Foster's kick into the end zone and a run out to the Eagles 18, the triple option got Dominique Swope free over right tackle and he went 82 yards for a touchdown. Mora's

extra point kick closed the game to 17–7.

A pop-up kickoff to Michael Williams got the Tide started on its 35, but Bama didn't seem to want to get started. Two false starts around a couple of poor plays had the Tide facing third-and-17 at the Bama 28 when McCarron found Gibson on the sideline. Gibson made a nice catch for a gain of 18 into Georgia Southern territory. From there it was a little bit of Lacy running to the Eagles 31 and then a dose of Richardson for all but a couple of yards for the rest of it. Richardson made a dive into the end zone for the touchdown and 24–7 Bama lead with 6:16 to play in the first half.

The Eagles weren't done. After another Cade Foster kickoff into the end zone (this one not returned), Georgia Southern started at its 20. The Eagles gave the Bama defense seven more looks at triple option runs (around a fourth down quarterback sneak for a first down). With the clock running to the one minute mark, the Eagles had the Bama defense suckered. Shaw faked the dive, then could take his choice of two Eagles receivers running behind the Alabama secondary. He threw it to Jonathan Bryant for the only Georgia Southern completion of the half and a 39-yard touchdown. With less than a minute to play the Tide lead had been cut to 24–14.

Bama made a last ditch drive, but it ended with three incomplete passes and a missed 47-yard field goal by Foster.

It looked as if Alabama might have a new resolve to start the second half. First, the Tide defense forced a punt. Then the offense made an excellent drive.

Starting at the Bama 15, Alabama went 85 yards in 10 plays. McCarron had a 16-yard pass to Marquis Maze to get the march started and then found Maze for 24 on a third-

Richardson works his way through the hole and into the Georgia Southern defensive backfield. No team scored more on Alabama in 2011 than the FCS Eagles, but they had no answer for the punishing rushing attack of the Crimson Tide.

and-13 play. On a second-and-10 from the Georgia Southern 34, McCarron had to scramble. He spotted a wide open tight end Brad Smelley at the five and hit him. Smelley stretched into the end zone for a touchdown with 7:17 remaining in the third quarter and the Tide had a 31–14 lead.

That little bit of breathing room lasted only 14 seconds as Georgia Southern return man Laron Scott took the kickoff at the five and raced 95 yards untouched for a touchdown, pulling the Eagles to within 31–21.

The Bama offense—which would not punt all day—had another drive ready to go, though. Bama went 74 yards in nine plays following the kickoff. McCarron had two nice passes on the drive. After a low snap to him in shotgun on a third-and-six, he got off a pass to Smelley, who made an excellent catch for a first down. Richardson then picked up 20 at right end, eight at left tackle, and three at right guard for a first down at the Georgia Southern 31. McCarron then hit Kevin Norwood for 22 and a first down at the Eagles nine.

It took Richardson two runs to get his third touchdown of the game and Alabama a 38–21 lead with just over four minutes remaining in the third quarter.

Basically, there would be only two more series in the game.

Georgia Southern kept the ball for eight minutes before a fourth-and-goal pass was broken up by DeQuan Menzie in the end zone.

Alabama then went on a 15-play, 92-yard drive that used up all but 44 seconds of the final quarter. It was mostly Richardson until the Tide got to midfield when Jalston Fowler took over at tailback. Fowler had a 12-yard run to get started and later in the drive on a third-and-eight would have a 22-yard run to the Georgia Southern two. Two plays later McCarron connected with Smelley for the touchdown and the final of 45–21. ■

Brad Smelley reaches for the end zone to score the final touchdown of the game. He had a pair of scores on his four catches, doubling his season scoring.

This Is Not First Rematch Rodeo

College football is regarded as having its beginning in 1869 when Rutgers defeated Princeton. The second game? Princeton demanded and received a rematch. So why the controversy now?

This year, Alabama earned a rematch in the BCS National Championship Game. LSU, undefeated at 13–0 and ranked No. 1 in the nation, and No. 2 Alabama, 11–1 with the one loss an overtime setback to LSU, met in the Louisiana Superdome on January 9 for the college football crown.

There are legitimate arguments against the BCS system of choosing a national champion in the biggest sport in America, major college football. What there is not an argument against is that the BCS met its mandate of matching the nation's two best college football teams. And there is nothing in the criteria regarding whether there is a rematch or whether the teams come from the same conference or whether a team has to be a conference champion to be national champion.

Two memorable bowl games were rematches, including one for the national championship. Once very rare, the rematch has become more common with conference championship games at the end of the season.

Alabama has played in one Southeastern Conference Championship Game rematch.

This year there were rematches in the Big Ten and ACC in the conference championship games, with varying results. In the Big Ten, Michigan State won the regular season game against Wisconsin, 37–31. In the rematch for the league championship, Wisconsin defeated the Spartans, 42–39. In the ACC, Clemson won both the regular season game (23–3) against Virginia Tech, and then the Tigers certified that win by taking a 38–10 win over the Hokies in the conference championship game.

Just a few years ago much of the nation was clamoring for a rematch. There could not be two better teams in America than No. 1 Ohio State and No. 2 Michigan, proclaimed many. The Buckeyes took a 42–39 win over the Wolverines in a game that was considered great, the lack of defense notwithstanding. But instead of a rematch, Florida was the number two team in the final BCS poll to meet Ohio State.

After giving up a touchdown on the opening kickoff, the Gators rolled to a 41–14 victory for the 2006 national championship.

A decade earlier, Florida had been involved in a rematch for the national championship. In the 1996 regular season, the Gators were ranked No. 1 and the Seminoles No. 2 going into the final regular season

After playing an all-time classic earlier in the year, the Bama-LSU rematch for the national championship was nothing new for college football, or even for the Alabama program.

game. FSU took a 24–21 win. They met again in the Sugar Bowl for the national championship, and Florida took a 52–20 win for the title.

That was the good rematch news for Coach Steve Spurrier.

The self-proclaimed, "Ball Coach" has the distinction of losing to a team in the regular season and again in the Southeastern Conference Championship Game twice.

In 1999, Coach Mike DuBose took his Alabama team to the swamp and came out with a 40–39 overtime win. The teams met again in the SEC title game and Bama romped to a 34–7 victory. Last year Spurrier was coach at South Carolina and his Gamecocks lost a close one at Auburn, 35–27, in regular season play. In the SEC Championship Game rematch, Spurrier again failed to show improvement, getting routed 56–17.

Most Alabama fans remember 1978 as the Crimson Tide winning the national championship with a win over No. 1 Penn State and Joe Paterno with a goalline stand in the Sugar Bowl, but there was another dynamic at work that season.

In early November, number four Nebraska hosted number one Oklahoma. The Sooners of Coach Barry Switzer had a five-game winning streak against the Cornhuskers of Coach Tom Osborne. But on this day, Oklahoma had two key fumbles and lost, 17–14. Missouri upset Nebraska a week later, making the Big Eight a three-way tie. There was a tie-in for the champion to go to the Orange Bowl, and the Orange Bowl elected to rematch Oklahoma and Nebraska. In the rematch, Oklahoma was a 31–24 winner.

Those are not the only rematches in college football. There is no pattern as to how the second game will play out.

Amazingly, none of those rematches has done anything to damage the success and popularity of college football. ■

Alabama has twice gotten the better of Steve Spurrier in rematches, and now LSU coach Les Miles can add his name to the list. Though the Tide lost the initial meeting between the teams, they won the more important contest.

Alabama Trounces Auburn, 42–14

For Sale! Owner No Longer Needs! "NEVER AGAIN" signs. Inquire University of Alabama Football Office. With a chance for its second national championship and 14th overall, the Crimson Tide put the disappointment of 2010 out of mind.

November 26

Alabama 42

@ Auburn 14

Alabama went to Auburn and routed the Tigers, 42–14. Alabama improved to 11–1 on the year, the lone loss an overtime 9–6 setback to LSU. Bama finishes 7–1 in SEC games. Auburn, a year after winning a national championship, fell to 7–5 overall, 4–4 in SEC games.

In one respect, the final score was misleading. Alabama's defense did not surrender a point. Auburn's two touchdowns were scored by the defense and by the kickoff return team.

A.J. McCarron had an exceptional game, passing for three touchdowns and completing 18 of 23 passes for 184 yards. Trent Richardson had 27 rushes for 203 yards, including a 57-yard run late in the fourth quarter that gave third team tailback Jalston Fowler the opportunity to tack on a a 15-yard touchdown run and close out the scoring.

Alabama was particularly effective in the first half with McCarron getting all of his touchdown passes. He also connected with tight end

Brad Smelley for six first half completions, including a touchdown. His other touchdown tosses went to Kenny Bell and to Richardson and he also had a two-point conversion pass to tight end Michael Williams.

The rout was reflected in the statistics. Alabama had 399 yards going to the final play of the game, when McCarron took a knee for a two-yard loss, leaving the Tide with just 397. But that was plenty more than the 140 total yards by Auburn, 45 of those coming on a final, futile drive.

Bama had 19 first downs to nine for Auburn. The Tide had 35 rushes for 213 yards, Auburn also 35 runs, but for only 78 yards. The Tigers were held to 11 of 20 passing for just 62 yards.

Auburn suffered one costly interception as Bama cornerback picked off a Clint Moseley pass and returned it 35 yards for a touchdown.

Alabama was led on defense by linebacker Dont'a Hightower, who was in on nine tackles (six primary) and one tackle for loss. Freshman Vinnie Sunseri played much of the game at safety

Trent Richardson rumbles ahead for some of his career-high 203 rushing yards, an exclamation point on a fine season that saw him deservedly invited to New York for the Heisman ceremony.

for Mark Barron and had a nice game with six tackles (four primary).

For the second consecutive year, Alabama had a 24–7 halftime lead. But it didn't seem much like last year's game—the one when the Tigers valuable quarterback Cam Newton brought Auburn back to a 28–27 win.

The Crimson Tide had dominated both sides of the line of scrimmage, the Tigers getting a touchdown on an offensive turnover and otherwise unable to move, unable to stop Alabama. And, specifically, unable to stop the McCarron-Smelley battery. McCarron was pitching and Smelley was catching like Auburn was North Texas or Georgia Southern. Smelley had four receptions against those two teams. Against Auburn in just the first two quarters, had a career high six receptions for a career high 86 yards. (Perhaps the Tigers made an adjustment, because Smelley did not have a second half catch.)

One of those Smelley receptions was a 35-yard first quarter touchdown, one of three first half touchdown completions by McCarron.

After the teams swapped three-and-outs, Bama started at its 11-yard line. On third-and-7 from the 22, Smelley caught a first down pass. Three plays later he had another first down catch.

There had been a lot of pregame talk about the trick plays of Auburn offensive coordinator Gus Malzahn, but it was Bama offensive coordinator Jim McElwain who drew first gadget blood. On a first-and-10 from the Auburn 41, Mc-Carron handed to Richardson, who turned and tossed it back to McCarron—a flea flicker. McCarron then hit a wide open Kenny Bell for the touchdown, the ninth play of the 81-yard drive. Jeremy Shelley kicked it to Alabama 7, Auburn 0 with 4:35 left in the first quarter.

Auburn had another three-and-out, followed by a shanked punt that went only 10 yards and set Bama up at the Tigers 35.

McCarron went back to Smelley. Alabama was in a three tight end formation with Smelley on the right side. He

The Alabama defense would stop at nothing, even if it meant losing their helmets, to beat down archrival Auburn in the Iron Bowl.

Quarterback Clint Moseley was ineffective at best for the Tigers and his tackling left something to be desired as Dee Milliner goes over the top to score on a fourth quarter interception return, all but sealing the win for Alabama.

crossed the field and was left unattended, catching the pass at the 10 and trotting in to make it 14–0 with 4:25 to play.

Auburn moved into Alabama territory—to the 49—on its next possession, where the Tigers faced fourth and three. It appeared Auburn might gamble, but instead AU quarterback Clint Moseley quick kicked to the 10.

Alabama wanted to pass and McCarron had protection, but couldn't find a receiver. Finally he was hit by defensive end Corey Lemonier and fumbled into the end zone. Kenneth Carter fell on the ball for Auburn for the touchdown. With four seconds remaining in the first quarter, Bama's lead had been cut to 7 at 14–7.

Alabama responded with a 12-play, 80-yard drive that was helped by an Auburn pass interference. McCarron completed third down passes for first downs to Bell (five yards), Smelley (six yards and 21 yards), and finished the drive with a five-yard pass to Trent Richardson. With 5:53 to play in the first half, Alabama had a 21–7 lead.

Auburn had another three-and-out on its next possession and Bama started at its 36. The drive included a 15-yard personal foul call against Auburn and a fourth down pass to Smelley for a first down, but the Tide couldn't get a touchdown, settling for a 30-yard Smelley field goal and a 24–7 lead with 1:44 to play.

Alabama's kickoff team, which has been mediocre to awful much of the year, bot an awful kickoff from Cade Foster to the 17 that was returned 83 yards by Onterio McCalebb through awful coverage for a touchdown that cut Bama's lead to 24–14 just 11 seconds into the second half.

Alabama responded, but not quite satisfactorily. Bama drove to a first down at the Auburn 12, but could cash only a field goal. After an Auburn kickoff to the end zone, Bama managed first downs on a seven-yard pass to Marquis Maze, a 35-yard Richardson run, and a 16-yard Richardson run. On second-and-nine the Tide was hit with a delay of game penalty, and ended up settling for Shelley's 28-yard field goal and a 27–14 lead.

Richardson lunges towards the pylon, but the Auburn tackler is able to force him down short of the goal line. Despite the career day, Richardson was unable to find the end zone in the final regular season game.

There would be no more scoring in the third quarter. For the most part, Alabama had poor field position owing to another nice kickoff return by McCalebb after Bama's field goal. But after Auburn failed on a fourth-and-one from the Alabama 47, Cody Mandell punted Auburn back to its nine on the final play of the third quarter.

That poor field position turned into a big Alabama play. The Tigers had two passes go incomplete, one that probably should have been intercepted by Dre Kirkpatrick. No problem.

The third Moseley pass was picked off by Tide cornerback Dee Milliner at the 35 and run back for a touchdown to make it 33–14. McCarron hit Williams on the two-point conversion with 14:38 to play in the game.

Auburn drove to a first-and-goal at the 10 and second and goal at the five, but the defense with a sack from Courtney Upshaw and a tackle on a scramble took over on downs at the 10.

It was no surprise that it would be Trent Richardson time, and he delivered with a performance that should enhance his Heisman Trophy chances.

He pulled Alabama out of the hole with a 13-yard run and two plays later went around left end, pounded a couple of defenders off him with stiff arms, and went back down the middle to the Auburn 16, a 57-yard run that put him over the 200-yard mark and ended his day.

Two plays later, Jalston Fowler went around right end and into the end zone.

Auburn's final offensive thrust ended with Moseley scrambling on a third and long and fumbling when tackled. At that time, Alabama had 399 yards of total offense to 140 for Auburn, but the Tide correctly took a knee to end the game, and fell short of 400 yards. ■

Not just excited to take home the win in the Iron Bowl, Alabama fans knew that the win over Auburn may have punched their ticket to a rematch with LSU for the national championship.

Even after the loss to LSU, Nick Saban never stopped believing in his team, knowing they had done more than enough to secure a shot at a second national championship in three years.